BEST-EVER
CHILLI COOKBOOK

BEST-EVER
CHILLI COOKBOOK

HOT AND SPICY DISHES FROM AROUND THE WORLD:
150 DELICIOUS RECIPES SHOWN IN 250 SIZZLING PHOTOGRAPHS

EDITED BY ELIZABETH YOUNG

HERMES HOUSE

This edition is published by Hermes House,
an imprint of Anness Publishing Ltd,
Hermes House,
88–89 Blackfriars Road,
London SE1 8HA;
tel. 020 7401 2077; fax 020 7633 9499

www.hermeshouse.com; www.annesspublishing.com

If you like the images in this book and would like
to investigate using them for publishing, promotions
or advertising, please visit our website
www.practicalpictures.com for more information.

Publisher: Joanna Lorenz
Editor: Elizabeth Young
Designer: Ian Sandom
Proofreading Manager: Lindsay Zamponi
Production Controller: Wendy Lawson

© Anness Publishing Ltd 2010

ETHICAL TRADING POLICY

At Anness Publishing we believe that business should
be conducted in an ethical and ecologically sustainable
way, with respect for the environment and a proper
regard to the replacement of the natural resources
we employ.

As a publisher, we use a lot of wood pulp in high-
quality paper for printing, and that wood commonly
comes from spruce trees. We are therefore currently
growing more than 750,000 trees in three Scottish
forest plantations: Berrymoss (130 hectares/320 acres),
West Touxhill (125 hectares/305 acres) and Deveron
Forest (75 hectares/185 acres). The forests we manage
contain more than 3.5 times the number of trees
employed each year in making paper for the books
we manufacture.

Because of this ongoing ecological investment
programme, you, as our customer, can have the pleasure
and reassurance of knowing that a tree is being
cultivated on your behalf to naturally replace the
materials used to make the book you are holding.

Our forestry programme is run in accordance with
the UK Woodland Assurance Scheme (UKWAS) and will
be certified by the internationally recognized Forest
Stewardship Council (FSC). The FSC is a non-
government organization dedicated to promoting
responsible management of the world's forests.
Certification ensures forests are managed in an
environmentally sustainable and socially responsible
way. For further information about this scheme, go to
www.annesspublishing.com/trees

PUBLISHER'S NOTE

Although the advice and information in this book are
believed to be accurate and true at the time of going to
press, neither the authors nor the publisher can accept
any legal responsibility or liability for any errors or
omissions that may be made nor for any inaccuracies
nor for any loss, harm or injury that comes about from
following instructions or advice in this book.

NOTES

For all recipes, quantities are given in both
metric and imperial measures and, where
appropriate, in standard cups and spoons.
Follow one set of measures, but not a mixture,
because they are not interchangeable.
Standard spoon and cup measures are level.
1 tsp = 5ml, 1 tbsp = 15ml, 1 cup = 250ml/8fl oz.
Australian standard tablespoons are 20ml.
Australian readers should use 3 tsp in place of
1 tbsp for measuring small quantities.
American pints are 16fl oz/2 cups. American
readers should use 20fl oz/2.5 cups in place of
1 pint when measuring liquids.
Electric oven temperatures in this book are for
conventional ovens. When using a fan oven, the
temperature will probably need to be reduced by
about 10–20°C/20–40°F. Since ovens vary, you
should check with your manufacturer's
instruction book for guidance.
The nutritional analysis given for each recipe is
calculated per portion (i.e. serving or item),
unless otherwise stated. If the recipe gives a
range, such as Serves 4–6, then the nutritional
analysis will be for the smaller portion size, i.e.
6 servings. Measurements for sodium do not
include salt added to taste.
Medium (US large) eggs are used unless
otherwise stated.

Contents

Introduction

Chillies are widely used to add flavour and interest to a variety of dishes, forming an important part of many of the world's major cuisines. They are also good for you, providing an excellent source of vitamin C and yielding beta carotene, folate, potassium and vitamin E.

HISTORICAL INFLUENCES

The word chilli is spelled in different ways. Sometimes it is chile, chili, or chilli pepper. This last description is accurate in that it recognizes that chillies are members of the *Capsicum genus*, like the sweet (bell) peppers. It also forms a link with all those spicy powders such as chilli, cayenne and paprika, which are an essential part of many national dishes

The great explorer Christopher Columbus was responsible for confusing chillies with peppercorns. When he set sail in 1492, hoping to find a sea route to the spice islands, it was a source of black pepper (*Piper nigrum*) he was seeking. Not only did he fail to find his intended destination, discovering instead the Caribbean island of San Salvador (now Watling Island), but he also assumed that the hot spice flavouring the local food was black pepper. By the time it was realized that the fleshy pods of a fruit were responsible, rather than black peppercorns, it was too late. The Spanish called the flavouring pimiento (pepper). The name stuck, and it has led to confusion ever since.

It was the Aztecs who coined the name chilli. Like the Mayas and Incas, they were greatly enamoured of the brightly coloured fruit that had originated in the rainforests of South America, and used chillies both as food and for medicinal purposes. When the Spanish invaded Mexico in 1509, they found many different varieties of both fresh and dried chilli. Mexico remains a mecca for those who love chillies, with every region having its own special varieties. Chillies are valued for their heat and for their flavour, and accomplished Mexican cooks will often use several different types in a single dish.

BELOW: *Fresh fruit such as fresh pineapple chunks are transformed into a red-hot, zesty dish when stir-fried with ginger and finely shredded chillies.*

ABOVE: *Spicy noodle soups can make a substantial and hearty meal.*

ABOVE: *Chilli salsas can be scorchingly hot, and are not for the faint-hearted.*

ABOVE: *Add jalapeño chillies to a dish if you enjoy very hot flavours.*

TYPES OF CHILLI

There are more than 200 different types of chillies, but those usually available include jalapeños, cayennes, Anaheim chillies and poblanos, as well as sweet (bell) peppers. Generally, small chillies are not hotter than big ones and red chillies are not hotter than green. Most chillies start out green and ripen to red, but some start yellow and become red, and yet others start yellow and stay yellow. Chillies on the same plant can have different degrees of heat, and in one type of chilli, the top of the fruit is hotter than the bottom. What makes one chilli hotter than another is the amount of the chemical capsaicin in the seeds and fibrous white lining. Capsaicin can produce a tingle or a tidal wave of heat, and also contributes to the feel-good factor by stimulating the brain to produce hormones called endorphins. A less appealing aspect to capsaicin is that it is an irritant, and can cause severe burning to delicate parts of the face and body with which it comes into contact, so it is vital to handle chillies with care. Wear gloves or cut them up using a knife and fork. If you do handle chillies directly, wash your hands in soapy water afterwards (capsaicin does not dissolve in water alone) or use vegetable oil to remove any residue.

USING THIS BOOK

Ideal for lovers of sizzling, hot food, this superb volume will increase the repertoire of any cook. The collection features a collection of 150 recipes to titillate your taste buds, featuring a variety of dishes from around the world, from subtly spiced to excitingly red-hot, all of which have been tested to ensure perfect results. Most of the recipes are intended for a family of four people, but the quantities can easily be halved to serve two, or doubled for eight. At the back of the book, there is a guide to the many types of chillies and chilli products, with tips for storing and preparing fresh and dried chillies.

Soups, stews and broths

Soups are a versatile dish. They can

be light and refreshing, warming and

filling, an appetizer to a main course

or even a meal in themselves.

The recipes in this chapter include

smooth and fiery vegetable soups,

scorching noodle broths and red-hot

stews flavoured with seafood, meat

and chicken, but they all share one

thing in common: lots of heat.

White radish and chilli broth

The red hot spicy flavours of the sliced chilli and ginger in this refreshing chilled soup are uniquely warming on a cold winter's night. A traditional Korean dish, this soup was served with sweet potatoes, which would have been baked in the embers of the household fire.

SERVES 4

3 Chinese white radishes, peeled
115g/4oz/¹/₂ cup salt
4 spring onions (scallions), shredded
1 garlic clove, sliced
115g/4oz fresh root ginger, sliced
2 red chillies, seeded and sliced
3 green chillies, seeded and sliced
1 Asian pear, peeled and diced
sugar syrup, to taste
10g/¹/₄oz/1 tbsp pine nuts, to garnish

1 Place the Chinese white radishes in a bowl. Pour in 3.5 litres/6 pints/ 15 cups water and the salt, and leave them to soak overnight.

2 The next day, add the spring onions to the radishes in salt water and leave them to stand for 30 minutes.

3 Tie the garlic and ginger in a muslin (cheesecloth) bag and add them to the radishes and spring onion with the red and green chillies.

4 Cover and leave to stand for another day in the refrigerator.

5 Remove the radishes from the mixture, cut them into bitesize dice and then return the pieces to the soup. Remove and discard the garlic and ginger.

6 Add the Asian pear to the soup. If the soup tastes a bit too salty, mix in a little sugar syrup. Garnish with pine nuts and serve.

Nutritional information per portion: Energy 48kcal/198kJ; Protein 1.7g; Carbohydrate 5.9g, of which sugars 5.8g; Fat 2.1g, of which saturates 0.2g; Cholesterol 0mg; Calcium 37mg; Fibre 2g; Sodium 28mg.

Spicy Tuscan soup

The origins of this classic, elegant cold Italian soup date back to the Medici court, and it is believed to have been created for banquets honouring guests from North Africa. Sizzling and delicious, this subtly spiced soup is perfect for serving on hot summer days.

SERVES 6

1/2 cucumber, peeled and cubed

1 fennel bulb, thinly sliced

1 celery heart, chopped

1 lettuce, chopped

4 tomatoes, peeled, seeded and chopped

3 carrots, quartered

1 lemon, peeled and thinly sliced

3 garlic cloves, chopped

1 dried red chilli, finely chopped

1 bunch fresh basil

75ml/2 1/2fl oz/1/3 cup extra virgin olive oil

sea salt and ground black pepper

croûtons, to serve (optional)

1 Place the cucumber, slices of fennel, chopped celery, lettuce, tomatoes, carrots, lemon, garlic, chilli and basil into a food processor.

2 Gradually process all ingredients until well mixed; alternatively, use a blender and blend until smooth.

3 Add 250ml/8fl oz/1 cup water and the extra virgin olive oil, then season with salt and black pepper to taste.

4 Ladle into a serving bowl and chill until required. Serve with croûtons, if you like.

Nutritional information per portion: Energy 119kcal/494kJ; Protein 1.3g; Carbohydrate 7.2g, of which sugars 6.9g; Fat 9.7g, of which saturates 1.4g; Cholesterol 0mg; Calcium 33mg; Fibre 2.9g; Sodium 23mg.

Gazpacho with chilli salsa

Tomatoes, cucumber, peppers and chilli form the basis of this sizzling version of the classic chilled soup. Add a spoonful of thickly chopped, fiery avocado salsa and a sprinkling of croûtons, and serve for a tasty light lunch or simple supper on a warm summer day.

SERVES 4

2 slices day-old white bread, cubed
600ml/1 pint/2¹/₂ cups chilled water
1kg/2¹/₄lb fresh tomatoes
1 cucumber
1 red (bell) pepper, halved, seeded
    and chopped
1 fresh green chilli, seeded and chopped
2 garlic cloves, chopped
30ml/2 tbsp extra virgin olive oil
juice of 1 lime and 1 lemon
a few drops of Tabasco sauce
salt and ground black pepper
8 ice cubes, to serve
a handful of basil leaves, to garnish

FOR THE CROÛTONS
2 slices day-old bread, crusts removed
1 garlic clove, halved
15ml/1 tbsp olive oil

FOR THE AVOCADO SALSA
1 ripe avocado
5ml/1 tsp lemon juice
2.5cm/1in piece cucumber, diced
¹/₂ red chilli, seeded and finely chopped

1 Place the cubed bread in a large bowl and pour over 150ml/¹/₄ pint/²/₃ cup of the water. Leave to soak for 5 minutes.

2 Meanwhile, place the tomatoes in a bowl and cover with boiling water. Leave for 30 seconds, then peel off the skin, remove the seeds and finely chop the flesh.

3 Thinly peel the skin off the cucumber, cut it in half lengthways and scoop out all the seeds with a teaspoon. Discard the inner part and chop the flesh into a fine dice.

4 Place the bread, tomatoes, cucumber, red pepper, chilli, garlic, olive oil, citrus juices and Tabasco in a food processor or blender with the remaining 450ml/³/₄ pint/scant 2 cups chilled water and blend until well combined but still chunky. Season to taste and chill for 2–3 hours.

5 To make the croûtons, rub the slices of bread with the garlic clove. Cut the bread into cubes and place in a plastic bag with the olive oil. Seal the bag and shake until the bread cubes are coated with the oil.

6 Heat a large non-stick frying pan and fry the croûtons over medium heat until crisp and golden.

7 Just before serving, make the avocado salsa. Halve the avocado, remove the stone (pit), then peel and dice. Toss the avocado in the lemon juice to prevent it from browning, then place it in a serving bowl and add the cucumber and chilli. Mix well.

8 Ladle the soup into four chilled bowls and add a couple of ice cubes to each one. Top each portion with a good spoonful of avocado salsa. Garnish with the basil and sprinkle the croûtons over the top of the salsa.

Nutritional information per portion: Energy 278Kcal/1166kJ; Protein 6.4g; Carbohydrate 32.2g, of which sugars 12.1g; Fat 14.6g, of which saturates 2.6g; Cholesterol 0mg; Calcium 80mg; Fibre 5.1g; Sodium 209mg.

Tomato and chilli soup with egg

This smouldering soup is popular in Vietnam and Cambodia. Served on its own with crusty bread, or accompanied with jasmine or ginger rice, this scorching dish makes a red-hot lunch.

SERVES 4

30ml/2 tbsp vegetable oil
3 shallots, finely sliced
2 garlic cloves, finely chopped
2 Thai chillies, seeded and finely sliced
25g/1oz galangal, shredded
8 large, ripe tomatoes, skinned, seeded
    and finely chopped
15ml/1 tbsp sugar
30ml/2 tbsp Thai fish sauce
4 lime leaves
900ml/1¹/₂ pints/3³/₄ cups chicken stock
15ml/1 tbsp wine vinegar
4 eggs
sea salt and ground black pepper

FOR THE GARNISH

chilli oil, for drizzling
1 small bunch fresh coriander (cilantro),
    finely chopped
1 small bunch fresh mint leaves,
    finely chopped

1 Heat the oil in a wok or heavy pan. Stir in the shallots, garlic, chillies and galangal and cook until golden and fragrant.

2 Add the tomatoes with the sugar, Thai fish sauce and lime leaves. Stir until it resembles a sauce. Pour in the stock and bring to the boil. Reduce the heat and simmer for 30 minutes. Season.

3 Just before serving, bring a wide pan of water to the boil. Add the vinegar and half a teaspoon of salt. Break the eggs into individual cups.

4 Stir the water rapidly to create a swirl and drop an egg into the centre of the swirl. Follow immediately with the others, or poach two at a time, and keep the water boiling to throw the whites up over the yolks.

5 Turn off the heat, cover the pan and leave to poach until firm enough to lift. Using a slotted spoon, lift the eggs out of the water and slip them into the hot soup. Drizzle a little chilli oil over the eggs, sprinkle with the coriander and mint, and serve.

Nutritional information per portion: Energy 181kcal/756kJ; Protein 8g; Carbohydrate 12.3g, of which sugars 11.5g; Fat 11.7g, of which saturates 2.4g; Cholesterol 190mg; Calcium 52mg; Fibre 2.3g; Sodium 280mg.

Fiery tomato soup with red pepper cream

Five fresh red chillies in this dazzling soup makes it red hot. If you prefer a milder and less spicy soup, simply reduce the number of chillies.

SERVES 4

1.5kg/3¼lb plum tomatoes, halved
5 red chillies, seeded
1 red (bell) pepper, halved and seeded
2 red onions, roughly chopped
6 garlic cloves, crushed
30ml/2 tbsp sun-dried tomato paste
45ml/3 tbsp olive oil
400ml/14fl oz/1⅔ cups vegetable stock
salt and ground black pepper
wild rocket (arugula) leaves, to garnish

FOR THE PEPPER CREAM
1 red (bell) pepper, halved and seeded
10ml/2 tsp olive oil
120ml/4fl oz/½ cup crème fraîche
few drops of Tabasco sauce

1 Preheat the oven to 200°C/400°F/Gas 6. Place the tomatoes, chillies, pepper, onions, garlic and tomato paste in a roasting pan. Drizzle with the oil and roast for 40 minutes.

2 Meanwhile, make the pepper cream. Lay the pepper halves skin side up on a baking tray and brush with the oil. Roast with the vegetables for about 30–40 minutes, until blistered. Transfer the pepper for the pepper cream to a bowl when cooked, cover with clear film (plastic wrap) and leave to cool.

3 Peel the skin from the pepper and purée the flesh in a food processor or blender with half the crème fraîche. Pour into a bowl and stir in the remaining crème fraîche. Season with salt and pepper and add a few drops of Tabasco. Process the roasted vegetables in batches, adding enough stock to each batch to make a thick purée.

4 Heat the soup gently and season well. Ladle the soup into bowls and spoon red pepper cream on top. Pile wild rocket leaves on top to garnish.

Nutritional information per portion: Energy 319Kcal/1330kJ; Protein 5.3g; Carbohydrate 23.5g, of which sugars 22g; Fat 23.4g, of which saturates 10g; Cholesterol 34mg; Calcium 67mg; Fibre 6.2g; Sodium 72mg.

Spicy red lentil soup with onion

This light lentil soup is flavoured with tomatoes and gets its fiery flavour from the fresh red chilli. The garnishes play an important role and can be served in a separate bowl.

SERVES 6

30–45ml/2–3 tbsp olive oil
1 large onion, finely chopped
2 garlic cloves, finely chopped
1 fresh red chilli, seeded and chopped
5–10ml/1–2 tsp cumin seeds
5–10ml/1–2 tsp coriander seeds
1 carrot, finely chopped
scant 5ml/1 tsp ground fenugreek
5ml/1 tsp sugar
15ml/1 tbsp tomato purée (paste)
250g/9oz/1 cup split red lentils
1.75 litres/3 pints/7½ cups
   chicken stock
salt and ground black pepper
1 small red onion, finely chopped,
   15ml/1 tbsp chopped fresh parsley,
   to garnish
4–6 lemon wedges, to serve

1 Heat the oil in a heavy pan and stir in the onion, garlic, chilli, cumin and coriander seeds. When the onion begins to colour slightly, toss in the carrot and cook for 2–3 minutes.

2 Add the fenugreek, sugar and tomato purée and stir in the lentils. Pour in the stock, stir well and bring to the boil.

3 Lower the heat, partially cover the pan with a lid and simmer for 30–40 minutes, until the lentils have broken up.

4 If the soup is too thick for your preference, thin it down to the desired consistency with a little water. Season with salt and pepper to taste.

5 Serve the soup as it is or, if you prefer a smooth texture, leave it to cool slightly, then blend it in a food processor or blender and reheat when ready to serve.

6 Ladle the soup into bowls and sprinkle liberally with the chopped onion and parsley. Serve with a wedge of lemon.

Nutritional information per portion: Energy 203kcal/856kJ; Protein 11.1g; Carbohydrate 31.8g, of which sugars 7.3g; Fat 4.4g, of which saturates 0.6g; Cholesterol 0mg; Calcium 45mg; Fibre 3.5g; Sodium 26mg.

Potato and peanut soup with red chillies

Peanut soup is a firm favourite throughout Central and South America. In this spicy soup, the ground nuts are used as a thickening agent, with unexpectedly delicious results.

SERVES 6

60ml/4 tbsp groundnut (peanut) oil
1 onion, finely chopped
2 garlic cloves, crushed
1 red (bell) pepper, seeded and chopped
250g/9oz potatoes, peeled and diced
2 fresh red chillies, seeded and chopped
200g/7oz canned chopped tomatoes
150g/5oz/1¼ cups unsalted peanuts
1.5 litres/2½ pints/6¼ cups beef stock
salt and ground black pepper
**30ml/2 tbsp chopped fresh coriander
    (cilantro), to garnish**

1 Heat the oil in a large heavy pan over low heat. Stir in the onion and cook for 5 minutes, until beginning to soften.

2 Add the garlic, pepper, potatoes, chillies and tomatoes. Stir well to coat the vegetables evenly in the oil, cover and cook for 5 minutes, until softened.

3 Meanwhile, toast the peanuts by gently cooking them in a large dry frying pan over medium heat. Keep moving the peanuts around the pan until they are evenly golden.

4 Set 30ml/2 tbsp of the peanuts aside, to use as garnish. Transfer the remaining peanuts to a food processor and process until finely ground. Add the vegetables and process again until smooth.

5 Return the mixture to the pan and stir in the beef stock. Bring to the boil, then lower the heat and simmer for 10 minutes.

6 Pour the soup into heated bowls. Garnish with a generous sprinkling of coriander and the remaining toasted peanuts.

Nutritional information per portion: Energy 260Kcal/1079kJ; Protein 8g; Carbohydrate 14.7g, of which sugars 6.2g; Fat 19.2, of which saturates 3.6g; Cholesterol 0mg; Calcium 30mg; Fibre 3g; Sodium 20mg.

Red-hot pumpkin and coconut soup

This sizzling soup is from Java, where it can be served on its own or as a spicy accompaniment to a poached or grilled fish dish. It is packed with vegetables and makes a satisfying vegetarian meal.

SERVES 4

30ml/2 tbsp palm, groundnut
  (peanut) or corn oil
150g/5oz pumpkin flesh
115g/4oz yard-long beans
220g/7¹/₂oz can bamboo shoots, drained
900ml/1¹/₂ pints coconut milk
10–15ml/2–3 tsp palm sugar (jaggery)
130g/4¹/₂oz fresh coconut, shredded
salt
cooked rice, to serve

FOR THE SPICE PASTE

4 shallots, chopped
25g/1oz fresh root ginger, chopped
4 red chillies, seeded and chopped
2 garlic cloves, chopped
5ml/1 tsp coriander seeds
4 candlenuts, toasted and chopped

1 Make the spice paste. Using a mortar and pestle, grind all the ingredients together to form a smooth paste, or blend them together in an electric blender or food processor.

2 Heat the oil in a wok or large, heavy pan, stir in the spice paste and fry until it smells fragrant. Toss the pumpkin, yard-long beans and bamboo shoots in the paste and pour in the coconut milk.

3 Add the palm sugar to the wok or pan and bring to the boil. Reduce the heat and cook for 5–10 minutes, until the vegetables are tender.

4 Season the soup with salt and pepper to taste and then stir in half the fresh shredded coconut. Ladle the soup into individual warmed bowls, sprinkle with the remaining coconut and serve with bowls of cooked rice to spoon the soup over.

Nutritional information per portion: Energy 333kcal/1388kJ; Protein 6g; Carbohydrate 26g, of which sugars 23.8g; Fat 23.6g, of which saturates 11.7g; Cholesterol 0mg; Calcium 115mg; Fibre 4.9g; Sodium 258mg.

Spicy parsnip soup

The mild sweetness of parsnips and mango chutney in this simple soup is given an exciting lift with a blend of chilli and spices, and is garnished with unusual sesame naan croûtons.

SERVES 4

30ml/2 tbsp olive oil
1 onion, chopped
1 garlic clove, crushed
1 small green chilli, seeded and chopped
15ml/1 tbsp grated fresh root ginger
5 large parsnips, diced
5ml/1 tsp cumin seeds
5ml/1 tsp ground coriander
2.5ml/1/2 tsp ground turmeric
30ml/2 tbsp mango chutney
1.2 litres/2 pints/5 cups water
juice of 1 lime
salt and ground black pepper
60ml/4 tbsp natural (plain) yogurt and
    mango chutney, to serve

FOR THE NAAN CROÛTONS

1 large naan
45ml/3 tbsp olive oil
15ml/1 tbsp sesame seeds

1 Heat the oil in a large pan and add the onion, garlic, chilli and ginger. Cook for 4–5 minutes, until the onion has softened and browned slightly. Add the parsnips and cook for 2–3 minutes. Sprinkle in the cumin seeds, coriander and turmeric and cook for 1 minute, stirring constantly.

2 Add the chutney and the water. Season well and bring to the boil. Reduce the heat and simmer for 15 minutes, until the parsnips are soft. Leave the soup to cool slightly. Process the cooled soup in a food processor or blender until smooth. Then return to the pan, and stir the lime juice into the soup.

3 For the naan croûtons, slice the naan into bitesize pieces. Heat the oil in a frying pan and cook the naan pieces until golden. Remove the pan from the heat and drain off any excess oil. Add the sesame seeds and return to the heat for 30 seconds, until the seeds are golden.

4 Ladle the soup into bowls. Add a little yogurt and top with mango chutney and sprinkle with the naan croûtons.

Nutritional information per portion: Energy 189Kcal/792kJ; Protein 4g; Carbohydrate 26.6g, of which sugars 15.5g; Fat 8.2g, of which saturates 1.2g; Cholesterol 0mg; Calcium 101mg; Fibre 7.5g; Sodium 110mg.

Fish soup with chilli

This warming and spicy soup is enriched with the flavours of lime and chilli. Two whole fish have been used to make the broth, but you could also make this with shellfish, if you like.

SERVES 6

2 litres/3¹/₂ pints/8 cups water

2 garlic cloves, very finely chopped

1 small red onion, finely chopped

1 spring onion (scallion), finely chopped

1 red chilli, seeded and finely chopped

30ml/2 tbsp finely chopped parsley

2 medium white fish, such as sea bass,
 about 1kg/2¹/₄lb total weight, cleaned
 and gutted

salt and ground black pepper

1 lime, sliced, to serve

1 Bring the water to the boil in a large pan with the garlic, red onion, and half the spring onion, chilli and parsley. When it bubbles, lay the fish in the pan. Season. Return to the boil, reduce the heat, cover and simmer for 10 minutes.

2 Lift out the fish and leave the soup simmering, uncovered, for a further 15–20 minutes.

3 Meanwhile, remove the heads and tails from the fish, take off the fillets and divide into individual portions. Keep warm.

4 Strain the soup and adjust the seasoning to taste. Divide the pieces of fish among hot bowls, pour over the soup, garnish with the reserved spring onion, chilli and parsley, and serve with slices of lime.

Nutritional information per portion: Energy 145kcal/610kJ; Protein 31g; Carbohydrate 1.1g, of which sugars 0.8g; Fat 1.9g, of which saturates 0.7g; Cholesterol 87mg; Calcium 63mg; Fibre 0.6g; Sodium 164mg.

Hot and spicy fish soup

White fish flakes are given a subtle bite of red chilli, and the watercress and spring onions add a refreshing quality. Halibut or sea bass work as well as cod.

SERVES 3–4

1 cod, filleted and skinned, head separate
225g/8oz Chinese white radish, peeled
1/2 onion, chopped
2 garlic cloves, crushed
22.5ml/4 1/2 tsp Korean chilli powder
5ml/1 tsp gochujang chilli paste
2 spring onions (scallions), roughly sliced
1 block firm tofu, cubed
90g/3 1/2oz watercress or
    rocket (arugula)
salt and ground black pepper

1 Slice the cod fillets into three or four large pieces and set the head aside. Cut the white radish into 2cm/3/4in cubes.

2 Bring 750ml/1 1/4 pints/3 cups water to the boil in large pan and add the fish head.

3 Add the radish, onion, crushed garlic and a pinch of salt to the pan. Then add the chilli powder and gochujang chilli paste.

4 Bring the pan to the boil for 5 minutes. Then remove the fish head and discard. Add the sliced cod fillet. Simmer until the fish is tender, about 4 minutes.

5 Add the spring onions, tofu, and watercress or rocket, and then simmer the soup without stirring for a further 2 minutes.

6 Season with salt and pepper, and serve the soup immediately.

Nutritional information per portion: Energy 132kcal/554kJ; Protein 23.4g; Carbohydrate 2.8g, of which sugars 2.3g; Fat 3g, of which saturates 0.5g; Cholesterol 46mg; Calcium 300mg; Fibre 1.1g; Sodium 80mg.

Tomato soup with squid and chilli

Asian-style squid seared with chillies mingles with the pungent tomato and garlic flavours of the Mediterranean in this wonderfully warming, rich and smooth soup.

SERVES 4

4 small squid (or 1–2 large squid)
60ml/4 tbsp olive oil
2 shallots, chopped
1 garlic clove, crushed
1.2kg/2½ lb ripe tomatoes,
   roughly chopped
15ml/1 tbsp sun-dried
   tomato paste

450ml/¾ pint/2 scant cups
   vegetable stock
about 2.5ml/½ tsp sugar
2 red chillies, seeded and chopped
30ml/2 tbsp chopped
   fresh tarragon
salt and ground black pepper
crusty bread, to serve

1 Wash the squid under cold water. Grasp the head and tentacles and pull the body away with the other hand. Discard the intestines that come away. Cut the tentacles away from the head in one piece and reserve; discard the head. Repeat with the remaining squid.

2 Pull the quills out of the main bodies of the squid and remove any roe. Pull off the fins from the body pouches and rub off the semi-transparent, mottled skin. Wash the squid under running cold water. Cut them into rings and set these aside with the tentacles.

3 Heat 30ml/2 tbsp of the oil in a heavy pan. Add the shallots and garlic, and cook for 4–5 minutes, until softened. Add the tomatoes and tomato paste. Season, cover and cook for 3 minutes. Add half the stock and simmer for 5 minutes, until the tomatoes are soft.

4 Cool the soup, then push it through a sieve (strainer) and return it to the rinsed-out pan. Stir in the remaining stock and sugar, and reheat gently.

5 Meanwhile, heat the remaining oil in a frying pan. Add the squid rings and tentacles, and the chillies. Cook for 4–5 minutes, stirring, then remove from the heat and stir in the tarragon.

6 Adjust the seasoning if necessary. If the soup tastes slightly sharp, add a little extra sugar. Ladle the soup into bowls and spoon the chilli squid in the centre. Serve with crusty bread.

Nutritional information per portion: Energy 186kcal/777kj; Protein 8.1g; Carbohydrate 10.9g; of which sugars 10.2g; Fat 12.6g; of which saturates 2g; Cholesterol 48mg; Calcium 30mg; Fibre 1.7g; Sodium 386mg.

Chilli crab soup

Prepared fresh crab is readily available and perfect for creating an exotic and fiery soup in minutes. This soup is simple to make and is filled with succulent and juicy crab meat.

SERVES 4

45ml/3 tbsp olive oil
1 red onion, finely chopped
2 red chillies, seeded and finely chopped
1 garlic clove, finely chopped
450g/1lb fresh white crab meat
30ml/2 tbsp chopped fresh parsley
30ml/2 tbsp chopped coriander (cilantro)
juice of 2 lemons
1 litre/1³⁄₄ pints/4 cups fish or
   chicken stock
15ml/1 tbsp Thai fish sauce
1 lemon grass stalk
150g/5oz vermicelli or angel hair pasta
salt and ground black pepper

FOR THE CORIANDER RELISH

50g/2oz/1 cup coriander (cilantro) leaves
1 green chilli, seeded and chopped
15ml/1 tbsp sunflower oil
25ml/1¹⁄₂ tbsp lemon juice
2.5ml/¹⁄₂ tsp ground roasted cumin seeds

1 Heat the oil in a pan and add the onion, chillies and garlic. Cook for 10 minutes until the onion is soft. Transfer to a bowl with the crab meat, parsley, coriander and lemon juice. Set aside.

2 Put the stock and fish sauce into a large heavy pan. Bruise the lemon grass, and add to the pan and bring to the boil.

3 Break the pasta into 5–7.5cm/ 2–3in lengths and stir it in. Simmer the pasta uncovered, for 3–4 minutes or cook for the time suggested on the packet, until the pasta is tender but al dente.

4 Meanwhile, make the coriander relish. Place the coriander, chilli, oil, lemon juice and cumin in a food processor or blender and process to form a coarse paste. Add seasoning to taste.

5 Remove and discard the lemon grass from the soup. Stir the chilli and crab mixture into the soup and season it well. Bring to the boil, then reduce the heat and simmer for 2 minutes.

6 Ladle the soup into four deep, warmed bowls and put a spoonful of the relish in the centre of each. Serve the soup immediately.

Nutritional information per portion: Energy 228kcal/951kj; Protein 23.6g; Carbohydrate 5.4g; of which sugars 5g; Fat 12.6g; of which saturates 6g; Cholesterol 90mg; Calcium 199mg; Fibre 1.1g; Sodium 767mg.

Spicy octopus and watercress soup

This refreshing seafood soup has a wonderfully restorative quality. Delicious octopus is cooked in a rich vegetable broth, with mooli and chilli adding an elusive and exotic flavour.

SERVES 2–3

1 large octopus, cleaned and gutted
150g/5oz mooli (daikon), peeled
1/2 leek, sliced
20g/3/4oz kelp or spinach leaves
3 garlic cloves, crushed
1 fresh red chilli, seeded and finely sliced
15ml/1 tbsp light soy sauce
75g/3oz watercress or rocket (arugula)
salt and ground black pepper

1 Rinse the octopus in salted water and cut into pieces about 2.5cm/1in long. Finely dice the mooli.

2 Pour 750ml/1¼ pints/3 cups water into a large heavy pan and bring to the boil.

3 Reduce the heat and add the mooli, leek, kelp or spinach, and crushed garlic. Simmer over medium heat until the mooli softens and becomes clear.

4 Remove and discard the kelp and leek from the pan and then add the sliced chilli.

5 Add the octopus, increase the heat and boil for 5 minutes. Season with soy sauce, salt and pepper, and then add the watercress or rocket.

6 Remove from the heat, cover the pan and leave to stand for 1 minute while the leaves wilt into the liquid. Ladle into bowls and serve.

Nutritional information per portion: Energy 106kcal/449kJ; Protein 19.9g; Carbohydrate 2.6g, of which sugars 2.3g; Fat 1.9g, of which saturates 0.5g; Cholesterol 48mg; Calcium 108mg; Fibre 1.7g; Sodium 386mg.

Chilli clam broth

This spicy soup of succulent clams in a chilli stock could not be easier to prepare. Popular in coastal areas of Colombia, it makes the perfect lunch on a hot summer's day.

SERVES 6

30ml/2 tbsp olive oil
1 onion, finely chopped
3 garlic cloves, crushed
2 fresh red chillies, seeded and
    finely chopped
250ml/8fl oz/1 cup dry white wine
400ml/14fl oz can plum tomatoes, drained
1 large potato, about 250g/9oz, peeled
    and diced

400ml/14fl oz/1²/₃ cups fish stock
1.3kg/3lb fresh clams
15ml/1 tbsp chopped fresh
    coriander (cilantro)
15ml/1 tbsp chopped fresh flat
    leaf parsley
salt
lime wedges, to serve

1 Heat the olive oil in a large pan. Add the chopped onion and sauté for 5 minutes over low heat until the onion has softened. Stir in the crushed garlic and chopped chillies and cook for a further 2 minutes. Pour in the wine and bring to the boil, then simmer for a further 2 minutes.

2 Add the plum tomatoes, diced potato and stock. Bring to the boil, cover and lower the heat to a simmer.

3 Season with salt and simmer for 15 minutes, until the potatoes are beginning to break up and the tomatoes have reduced to a thick, rich sauce.

4 Meanwhile, wash the clams thoroughly under cold running water. Gently tap any that are open, and discard any clams that do not close when tapped.

5 Add the washed clams to the soup, cover and cook for about 3–4 minutes, or until the clams have opened. Discard any that do not open. Stir in the herbs and season to taste.

6 Check over the clams and throw away any that have failed to open. Ladle the soup into warmed bowls. Offer the lime wedges separately, to be squeezed over the soup just before eating.

Nutritional information per portion: Energy 278Kcal/1166kJ; Protein 6.4g; Carbohydrate 32.2g, of which sugars 12.1g; Fat 14.6g, of which saturates 2.6g; Cholesterol 0mg; Calcium 80mg; Fibre 5.1g; Sodium 209mg.

Chilli seafood stew with udon noodles

Spicy seasoning and thick Japanese udon noodles are added to this chilli and garlic-infused stew to create an enticing and fiery dish. Add a bowl of steamed rice for a perfect quick lunch.

SERVES 2

50g/2oz pork loin

50g/2oz mussels

50g/2oz prawns (shrimp)

90g/3½oz squid

15ml/1 tbsp vegetable oil

1 dried chilli, sliced

½ leek, sliced

2 garlic cloves, finely sliced

5ml/1 tsp grated fresh root ginger

30ml/2 tbsp Korean chilli powder

5ml/1 tsp mirin or rice wine

50g/2oz bamboo shoots, sliced

½ onion, roughly chopped

50g/2oz carrot, roughly chopped

2 Chinese leaves (Chinese cabbage),
    roughly chopped

750ml/1¼ pints/3 cups beef stock

light soy sauce, to taste

300g/11oz udon or flat wheat noodles

salt

1 Slice the pork, and set aside. Scrub the mussels' shells and rinse under water. Discard any that remain open after being tapped. Scrape off any barnacles and remove the 'beards'. Rinse well. Gently pull the tail shells from the prawns and remove the head. Peel the body shells and rinse well.

2 Wash and prepare the squid. Rinse the pouch and tentacles well under cold running water. Score the flesh in a criss-cross pattern, and slice into 2cm/¾in pieces.

3 Heat a large pan with the oil. Add the chilli, leek, garlic and ginger. Fry until the garlic has browned and add the pork. Fry the pork quickly, then add the chilli powder and mirin or rice wine. Add the bamboo shoots, onion and carrot, and continue to fry until the vegetables have softened.

4 Add the rinsed seafood and chopped cabbage and cook for 30 seconds. Pour in the stock and bring to the boil, then cover and simmer for 3 minutes. Season with salt. Discard any closed mussels.

5 Cook the udon noodles in a large pan of boiling water. Drain, then place the noodles in individual soup bowls and ladle over the soup. Serve the stew immediately while hot.

Nutritional information per portion: Energy 778kcal/3288kJ; Protein 39.5g; Carbohydrate 122.8g, of which sugars 9.4g; Fat 17.7g, of which saturates 1.4g; Cholesterol 176mg; Calcium 104mg; Fibre 6.9g; Sodium 734mg.

Spicy chicken broth

A delicious and warming chilli-infused broth originating from the Philippines. Traditionally it is served with steamed rice, but is also sipped during the meal to cleanse and stimulate the palate.

SERVES 4–6

15–30ml/1–2 tbsp palm or groundnut (peanut) oil

2 garlic cloves, finely chopped

1 large onion, sliced

40g/1¹/₂oz fresh root ginger, finely grated

2 whole dried chillies

1 chicken, left whole or jointed, trimmed of fat

30ml/2 tbsp Thai fish sauce

600ml/1 pint/2¹/₂ cups chicken stock

1.2 litres/2 pints/5 cups water

1 small green papaya, cut into fine slices or strips

1 bunch fresh young chilli or basil leaves

salt and ground black pepper

cooked rice, to serve

1 Heat the oil in a large pan that has a lid. Stir in the garlic, onion and ginger and fry until they begin to colour and soften. Stir in the dried chillies, add the chicken and fry until the skin is lightly browned all over.

2 Pour in the fish sauce, stock and water, adding more water if necessary so that the whole chicken is completely covered.

3 Bring to the boil, reduce the heat, cover and simmer gently for about 1¹/₂ hours, until the chicken is tender when pierced with a knife.

4 Season the stock with salt and pepper and add the papaya slices. Simmer for 10–15 minutes, then stir in the chilli or basil leaves, reserving some leaves to garnish. Serve the chicken and broth over warmed bowls of steamed rice.

Nutritional information per portion: Energy 132kcal/554kJ; Protein 23.4g; Carbohydrate 2.8g, of which sugars 2.3g; Fat 3g, of which saturates 0.5g; Cholesterol 46mg; Calcium 300mg; Fibre 1.1g; Sodium 80mg.

Chicken and rice soup with chilli

This tasty soup is Cambodia's answer to the chicken noodle soup. Light and refreshing with a hint of chilli, it is the perfect choice for a hot day, and a great pick-me-up when you are feeling tired.

SERVES 3–4

2 lemon grass stalks, trimmed
15ml/1 tbsp Thai fish sauce
90g/3½oz/½ cup short grain rice
salt and ground black pepper
1 small bunch coriander (cilantro)
   leaves, finely chopped, and 1 green
   or red chilli, seeded and cut into
   thin strips, to garnish
1 lime, cut in wedges, to serve

FOR THE STOCK

1 small chicken or 2 meaty chicken
   legs portions
1 onion, quartered
2 garlic cloves, crushed
25g/1oz fresh root ginger, sliced
2 lemon grass stalks
2 dried red chillies
30ml/2 tbsp Thai fish sauce

1 Put the chicken into a large pan with a lid. Add all the other stock ingredients and pour in 2 litres/3½ pints/8 cups water. Bring the stock to the boil, then reduce the heat and simmer, and cover with the lid, for 2 hours.

2 Skim any fat from the surface of the stock. Strain and keep the stock to one side. Take the chicken out of the pan and remove the skin from the chicken and then shred the meat. Set the shredded meat aside.

3 Pour the strained stock back into the pan and bring to the boil, then simmer.

4 Cut the lemon grass in half lengthways, then into three smaller pieces, and lightly bruise. Add it to the stock with the Thai fish sauce and the rice and simmer, uncovered, for 40 minutes. Add the shredded chicken and season.

5 Ladle the hot soup into bowls, garnish with the coriander and strips of chilli and serve with lime wedges to squeeze over.

Nutritional information per portion: Energy 147kcal/615kJ; Protein 12.8g; Carbohydrate 19.8g, of which sugars 1.4g; Fat 1.7g, of which saturates 0.4g; Cholesterol 53mg; Calcium 37mg; Fibre 0.8g; Sodium 320mg.

Spicy Chicken and noodle soup

This delicious and fiery noodle soup originated in Burma, but it is now one of the signature dishes of the city of Chiang Mai, Thailand. It is also the Thai equivalent of the famous Malaysian laksa.

SERVES 4–6

600ml/1 pint/2½ cups coconut milk
30ml/2 tbsp Thai red curry paste
5ml/1 tsp ground turmeric
450g/1lb chicken thighs, boned and cut
    into bitesize chunks
600ml/1 pint/2½ cups chicken stock
60ml/4 tbsp Thai fish sauce
15ml/1 tbsp dark soy sauce
juice of ½–1 lime
450g/1lb fresh egg noodles, blanched
    briefly in boiling water
salt and ground black pepper

TO GARNISH

3 spring onions (scallions), chopped
4 fresh red chillies, chopped
4 shallots, chopped
60ml/4 tbsp sliced pickled mustard
    leaves, rinsed
30ml/2 tbsp fried sliced garlic
coriander (cilantro) leaves
4–6 fried noodle nests (optional)

1 Pour about one-third of the coconut milk into a large, heavy pan or wok. Bring to the boil over medium heat, stirring frequently with a wooden spoon until the milk separates.

2 Add the red curry paste and ground turmeric, and stir to mix completely and cook until the mixture is fragrant. Add the chunks of chicken and toss over the heat for about 2 minutes, making sure that they are thoroughly coated with the curry paste.

3 Add the remaining coconut milk, the chicken stock, fish sauce and soy sauce. Season with salt and pepper to taste. Bring to simmering point, stirring frequently, then lower the heat and cook gently for 7–10 minutes. Remove from the heat and stir in lime juice to taste.

4 Reheat the fresh egg noodles in boiling water, drain and divide among four to six warmed bowls. Divide the chunks of chicken among the bowls and ladle in the hot soup. Top each serving with spring onions, chillies, shallots, pickled mustard leaves, fried garlic, coriander leaves and a fried noodle nest, if using. Serve immediately.

Nutritional information per portion: Energy 606kcal/2569kj; Protein 39.5g; Carbohydrate 88.7g; of which sugars 10.1g; Fat 12.9g; of which saturates 3.7g; Cholesterol 135mg; Calcium 84mg; Fibre 3.3g; Sodium 1111mg.

Spicy garlic and pork soup

This warming and sustaining rice soup can be made with pork or chicken. Sliced chillies are added to this meaty soup when it is ready to be served, to give it an extra kick.

SERVES 4 – 6

15–30ml/1–2 tbsp groundnut (peanut) oil

1 large onion, finely chopped

2 garlic cloves, finely chopped

25g/1oz fresh root ginger, finely chopped

350g/12oz pork rump or tenderloin, cut widthways into bitesize slices

5–6 black peppercorns

115g/4oz/1 cup plus 15ml/1 tbsp short grain rice

2 litres/3½ pints/8 cups chicken stock

30ml/2 tbsp fish sauce

salt

2 garlic cloves, finely chopped, to serve

2 spring onions (scallions), white parts only, finely sliced, to serve

2–3 green or red chillies, seeded and quartered lengthways, to serve

1 Heat the oil in a wok or deep, heavy pan that has a lid. Stir in the chopped onion, garlic and ginger and fry until fragrant and beginning to colour. Add the pork and fry, stirring frequently, for 5–6 minutes, until lightly browned. Stir in the black peppercorns.

2 Meanwhile, put the rice in a sieve (strainer), rinse under cold running water until the water runs clear, then drain. Toss the rice into the pan, making sure that it is coated in the mixture.

3 Pour in the stock, add the fish sauce and bring to the boil. Reduce the heat and partially cover with a lid. Simmer for 40 minutes, stirring ocassionally to make sure that the rice doesn't stick to the bottom of the pan. Season with salt to taste.

4 Just before serving, dry-fry the garlic in a small, heavy pan until golden brown, then stir it into the soup. Ladle the soup into individual warmed bowls and sprinkle the spring onions and sliced chillies over the top.

Nutritional information per portion: Energy 195kcal/813kJ; Protein 14.8g; Carbohydrate 19.9g, of which sugars 3.4g; Fat 6.2g, of which saturates 1.3g; Cholesterol 37mg; Calcium 24mg; Fibre 0.8g; Sodium 399mg.

Chilli lamb broth

This filling and hearty soup makes a great supper dish. It contains chunks of lamb that are slowly stewed in a chilli paste until it is extremely tender. Serve with chunks of crusty bread.

SERVES 4–6

25g/1oz fresh root ginger, peeled
   and chopped
4–6 garlic cloves, chopped
1 red chilli, seeded and chopped
15ml/1 tbsp ghee or vegetable oil
5ml/1 tsp coriander seeds
5ml/1 tsp cumin seeds
5ml/1 tsp ground fenugreek
5ml/1 tsp sugar
450g/1lb meaty lamb ribs, chopped
   into bitesize pieces
2 litres/3½ pints/8 cups lamb stock
   or water
10ml/2 tsp tomato purée (paste)
1 cinnamon stick
4–6 cardamom pods, bruised
2 tomatoes, peeled and quartered
salt and ground black pepper
fresh coriander (cilantro) leaves, roughly
   chopped, to garnish

1 Using a mortar and pestle or a food processor, grind the ginger, garlic and chilli to a paste.

2 Heat the ghee or oil in a heavy pan and stir in the coriander and cumin seeds.

3 Add the ginger, garlic and chilli paste along with the fenugreek and sugar. Stir until fragrant and beginning to colour. Add the lamb, searing the meat on both sides.

4 Pour in the stock or water and stir in the tomato purée, cinnamon stick and cardamom pods.

5 Bring to the boil, then reduce the heat, cover the pan and simmer gently for about 1½ hours, until the meat is tender.

6 Season to taste with salt and pepper. Stir in the tomatoes, and garnish with coriander. Serve hot with chunks of fresh crusty bread.

Nutritional information per portion: Energy 166kcal/693kJ; Protein 15.2g; Carbohydrate 2.8g, of which sugars 2.5g; Fat 10.6g, of which saturates 5.2g; Cholesterol 62mg; Calcium 12mg; Fibre 0.5g; Sodium 87mg.

Spicy beef noodle soup

This classic noodle soup is a Vietnamese family favourite. It is simple to prepare and makes a satisfying meal. If you want to set your taste buds alight, add sliced chillies to the stock.

SERVES 6

2 litres/3½ pints/8 cups good-quality
    beef stock
500g/1¼lb dried rice noodles, soaked
    for 20 minutes
250g/9oz beef sirloin
1 onion
6–8 spring onions (scallions)
2–3 red Thai chillies
115g/4oz/½ cup beansprouts
1 large bunch each fresh coriander
    (cilantro) and mint, stalks removed,
    leaves chopped, to garnish
2 limes, cut in wedges (optional), to serve

1 Put the beef stock in a large pan and bring to the boil. Reduce to a low heat and leave to simmer until ready to use.

2 Bring a pan of water to the boil. Drain the soaked rice noodles and add to the boiling water. Cook the noodles for about 4 minutes or until soft and tender. Drain the rice noodles and divide them among six wide soup bowls.

3 Thinly slice the beef sirloin across the grain. Halve and finely slice the onion, and cut the spring onions into long pieces. Slice the red chillies in half lengthways, and use a knife and fork to carefully scrape out and discard all the seeds. Continue to finely slice the rest of the chillies.

4 Divide the sliced beef, onion, spring onion pieces, chillies and beansprouts into six portions and place in the soups bowls on top of the rice noodles.

5 Ladle the beef stock on top of the noodles and garnish with the freshly chopped herbs. Serve immediately while hot.

Nutritional information per portion: Energy 391kcal/1635kJ; Protein 16g; Carbohydrate 74g, of which sugars 3g; Fat 2g, of which saturates 1g; Cholesterol 21mg; Calcium 62mg; Fibre 0.8g; Sodium 600mg.

Chilli beef and aubergine soup

This wonderful soup is sweet, spicy and tangy, flavoured with the Cambodian herbal condiment kroeung and fish sauce. The combination of fresh and dried chillies gives this dish extra fire.

SERVES 6

4 dried chillies
15ml/1 tbsp vegetable oil
75ml/5 tbsp kroeung
2–3 fresh red chillies
75ml/5 tbsp tamarind extract
15–30ml/1–2 tbsp Thai fish sauce
30ml/2 tbsp palm sugar (jaggery)
12 Thai aubergines (eggplants), stems
    removed, cut into chunks
1 bunch watercress or rocket (arugula),
    trimmed and chopped
1 handful fresh curry leaves
sea salt and ground black pepper

FOR THE STOCK

1kg/2¼lb beef shanks or brisket
2 large onions, quartered
2–3 carrots, cut into chunks
90g/3½oz fresh root ginger, sliced
5ml/1 tsp black peppercorns
30ml/2 tbsp soy sauce
45–60ml/3–4 tbsp Thai fish sauce

1 To make the stock, put the beef shanks or brisket into a pan with the other stock ingredients except the soy sauce and fish sauce. Add 3 litres/5 pints/ 12 cups water and bring to the boil, then simmer, covered, for 2–3 hours.

2 Soak the dried chillies in water for 30 minutes. Split them open, remove the seeds and scrape out the pulp. Stir the soy sauce and fish into the stock. Simmer, uncovered, for another hour, to reduce to about 2 litres/3½ pints/7¾ cups. Skim and strain. Tear half the meat into strips and reserve.

3 Heat the oil in a wok and stir in the kroeung, the pulp from the dried chillies and the whole fresh chillies. Stir until the mixture darkens.

4 Add the tamarind extract, fish sauce, sugar and stock. Stir well and bring to the boil. Reduce the heat and add the beef, aubergines and watercress or rocket. Cook for 20 minutes to allow the flavours to mingle.

5 Meanwhile, heat a pan, add the curry leaves and dry-fry them until they begin to crackle. Season the soup to taste, stir in half the curry leaves and ladle into bowls. Sprinkle the remaining curry leaves over the top and serve.

Nutritional information per portion: Energy 303kcal/1276kJ; Protein 37g; Carbohydrate 16.5g, of which sugars 14.5g; Fat 10.6g, of which saturates 4.2g; Cholesterol 90mg; Calcium 35mg; Fibre 2.4g; Sodium 300mg.

Mexican beef chilli soup with Monterey Jack nachos

Steaming bowls of fiery meaty soup, packed with beans, are delicious topped with crushed tortillas and cheese. Pop the bowls under the grill to melt the cheese, if you wish.

SERVES 4

45ml/3 tbsp olive oil
350g/12oz rump steak, cut into
   small pieces
2 onions, chopped
2 garlic cloves, crushed
2 green chillies, seeded and
   finely chopped
30ml/2 tbsp mild chilli powder
5ml/1 tsp ground cumin
2 bay leaves
30ml/2 tbsp tomato purée (paste)

900ml/1¹/₂ pints/3³/₄ cups beef stock
2 x 400g/14oz cans mixed beans,
  drained and rinsed
45ml/3 tbsp chopped fresh coriander
  (cilantro) leaves
salt and ground black pepper

FOR THE TOPPING
bag of plain tortilla chips, lightly crushed
225g/8oz/2 cups Monterey Jack or
   Cheddar cheese, grated

1 Heat the oil in a large pan over high heat and cook the steak pieces until they are golden all over. Use a slotted spoon to remove them from the pan.

2 Reduce the heat and add the onions, garlic and chillies, then cook for 4–5 minutes, until softened.

3 Add the chilli powder and ground cumin, and cook for a further 2 minutes. Return the meat to the pan, then stir in the bay leaves, tomato purée and beef stock, and bring the mixture to the boil. Reduce the heat, cover the pan and simmer for about 45 minutes, or until the meat is tender.

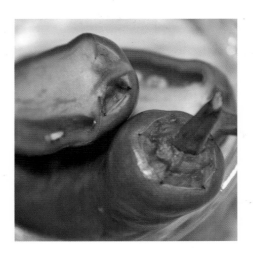

4 Put a quarter of the beans into a bowl and mash with a potato masher. Stir the mashed beans into the soup to thicken it slightly. Add the remaining beans and simmer for about 5 minutes. Season and stir in the chopped coriander. Ladle the soup into warmed bowls and spoon tortilla chips on top. Pile grated cheese over the tortilla chips and serve.

Nutritional information per portion: Energy 749Kcal/3135kJ; Protein 50g; Carbohydrate 54.1g, of which sugars 10.3g; Fat 37.2g, of which saturates 16.1g; Cholesterol 106mg; Calcium 609mg; Fibre 14.5g; Sodium 1473mg.

Dips, salsas, appetizers and snacks

This chapter shows just how versatile chillies can be, with an assortment of sizzling dips and salsas that will add a tangy sweetness and spice to any dish. With flavours ranging from the Mediterranean to South America, you'll discover a new world of fiery appetizers and snacks, all of which will get your tastebuds tingling.

Chunky guacamole with chilli

A popular and well-loved avocado-based dish that originated in Mexico. It is a delicious dip on its own or makes a super-spicy accompaniment for grilled fish, poultry or meat.

SERVES 4

2 large ripe avocados
1 small red onion, very finely chopped
1 red or green chilli, seeded and very
   finely chopped
¹/₂–1 garlic clove, crushed with a
   little salt (optional)
finely shredded rind of ¹/₂ lime and juice
   of 1–1¹/₂ limes
pinch of caster (superfine) sugar
225g/8oz tomatoes, seeded and chopped
30ml/2 tbsp roughly chopped
   fresh coriander (cilantro)
2.5–5ml/¹/₂–1 tsp ground toasted
   cumin seeds
15ml/1 tbsp olive oil
15–30ml/1–2 tbsp sour cream
salt and ground black pepper
lime wedges, dipped in sea salt, and fresh
   coriander sprigs, to garnish

1 Halve, stone (pit) and peel the avocados. Set one half aside and roughly mash the remainder in a bowl using a fork.

2 Add the onion, chilli, garlic (if using), lime rind, juice of 1 lime, sugar, tomatoes and coriander. Add ground cumin and seasoning. Stir in the olive oil.

3 Dice the remaining avocado half and stir into the guacamole mixture. Cover the bowl and leave the mixture to stand for 15 minutes so that the flavour develops. Then stir in the sour cream.

4 Serve immediately with lime wedges, dipped in sea salt, and coriander sprigs.

Nutritional information per portion: Energy 244kcal/1010kJ; Protein 8.8g; Carbohydrate 4.4g, of which sugars 4.3g; Fat 21.4g, of which saturates 8.5g; Cholesterol 35mg; Calcium 205mg; Fibre 0.7g; Sodium 731mg.

Spicy pumpkin dip

This tasty dip gets its kick from the mixture of spices and sliced chilli. Use jalapeño or serrano for a seriously hot dish. Serve it with chunks of bread or raw vegetables to dip into it.

SERVES 6–8

45–60ml/3–4 tbsp olive oil

1 onion, finely chopped

5–8 garlic cloves, roughly chopped

675g/1½lb pumpkin, peeled and diced

5–10ml/1–2 tsp ground cumin

5ml/1 tsp paprika

1.5–2.5ml/¼–½ tsp ground ginger

1.5–2.5ml/¼–½ tsp curry powder

75g/3oz chopped canned tomatoes or
    diced fresh tomatoes and 15–30ml/
    1–2 tbsp tomato purée (paste)

½–1 red jalapeño or serrano
    chilli, chopped

pinch of sugar, if necessary

juice of ½ lemon, or to taste

salt

30ml/2 tbsp chopped fresh coriander
    (cilantro) leaves, to garnish

1 Heat the oil in a frying pan, add the onion and half the garlic and fry until softened.

2 Add the diced pumpkin, then cover the pan and cook for about 10 minutes, or until half-tender.

3 Add the cumin, paprika, ground ginger and curry powder to the pan and cook for 1–2 minutes.

4 Stir in the tomatoes, chilli, sugar and salt and cook over medium heat until the liquid has evaporated.

5 When the pumpkin is tender, mash to a paste. Add the remaining garlic and season, then stir in the lemon juice.

6 Leave the dip to cool and sprinkle with the chopped fresh coriander.

Nutritional information per portion: Energy 54kcal/224kJ; Protein 0.9g; Carbohydrate 2.9g; of which sugars 2.3g; Fat 4.4g; of which saturates 0.7g; Cholesterol 1mg; Calcium 37mg; Fibre 1.3g; Sodium 3mg.

Chilli yogurt cheese balls

The cheese is bottled in extra virgin olive oil with dried chillies and fresh herbs to make an aromatic appetizer. It is delicious spread on thick slices of toast as a snack or a light lunch.

FILLS TWO 450G/1LB JARS

1 litre/1³/₄ pints/4 cups Greek sheep's (US strained plain) yogurt

10ml/2 tsp crushed dried chillies or chilli powder

30ml/2 tbsp chopped fresh herbs, such as rosemary, and thyme or oregano

about 300ml/¹/₂ pint/1¹/₄ cups extra virgin olive oil, preferably garlic-flavoured

toasted bread, to serve

1 Sterilize a 30cm/12in square of muslin (cheesecloth) by soaking it in boiling water. Drain and lay it over a large plate. Season the yogurt with salt and spoon it on to the centre of the muslin. Tie firmly with string.

2 Hang the muslin bag in a suitable position where it can be suspended over a large bowl to catch the whey. Leave for 2–3 days until the yogurt stops dripping. Sterilize two 450g/1lb glass preserving or jam jars by heating them in the oven at 150°C/300°F/Gas 2 for 15 minutes.

3 Mix the crushed dried chillies or chilli powder with the chopped herbs. Take teaspoonfuls of the cheese and roll them into balls with your hands. Lower into the jars, sprinkling each layer with the herb mixture. Pour the oil over the cheese until covered. Store in the refrigerator for up to 3 weeks.

4 To serve, spoon out the cheese and spread on slices of toasted bread.

Nutritional information per portion: Energy 1331kcal/5488kJ; Protein 24g; Carbohydrate 7.5g, of which sugars 7.5g; Fat 138.2g, of which saturates 33.8g; Cholesterol 0mg; Calcium 563mg; Fibre 0g; Sodium 758mg.

Feta and roast pepper dip with chillies

This is a familiar meze in northern Greece, where it is eaten as a dip with pittas. The feta cheese with the smoky peppers and hot chillies makes a powerful combination to enliven the tastebuds.

SERVES 4

1 yellow or green (bell) pepper
1–2 fresh green chillies
200g/7oz feta cheese
60ml/4 tbsp extra virgin olive oil
juice of 1 lemon
45–60ml/3–4 tbsp milk
ground black pepper
a little finely chopped fresh flat leaf
 parsley, to garnish
slices of toasted Greek bread or pittas,
 to serve

1 Thread the pepper and the chillies on metal skewers and turn them over a flame or under the grill (broiler), until the skins are charred.

2 Put the pepper and chillies in a plastic bag or in a covered bowl and set them aside until cool enough to handle. Peel off the pepper and chilli skins and wipe the blackened bits off. Slit the pepper and chillies and discard the seeds and stems.

3 Put the pepper and chilli flesh into a food processor. Add all the other ingredients except the parsley and blend to a fairly smooth paste. Add a little more milk if the mixture seems too stiff. Spread on slices of toast, sprinkle a little parsley on top and serve.

Nutritional information per portion: Energy 244kcal/1010kJ; Protein 8.8g; Carbohydrate 4.4g, of which sugars 4.3g; Fat 21.4g, of which saturates 8.5g; Cholesterol 35mg; Calcium 205mg; Fibre 0.7g; Sodium 731mg.

Salsa verde

There are many versions of this spicy and rustic Italian sauce. This is a classic green salsa in which capers play an important part. Make it with green cayenne chillies or the milder jalapeños.

SERVES 4

2–4 green chillies, halved and seeded
8 spring onions (scallions), chopped
   into long pieces
2 garlic cloves, halved
50g/2oz salted capers
sprig of fresh tarragon
bunch of fresh parsley
grated rind and juice of 1 lime
juice of 1 lemon
90ml/6 tbsp olive oil
about 15ml/1 tbsp green Tabasco sauce
ground black pepper

1 Place the chillies, spring onions and garlic cloves in a food processor or blender and process briefly.

2 Use your fingers to rub the excess salt off the capers. Add them, with the tarragon and parsley, to the food processor and pulse again until the ingredients are quite finely chopped.

3 Transfer the mixture to a bowl. Mix in the lime rind and juice, lemon juice and olive oil, stirring lightly so the citrus juice and oil do not emulsify. Add green Tabasco sauce, a little at a time, and black pepper to taste. Chill the salsa in the refrigerator until ready to serve.

Nutritional information per portion: Energy 158kcal/652kJ; Protein 0.9g; Carbohydrate 1.1g, of which sugars 1g; Fat 16.8g, of which saturates 2.4g; Cholesterol 0mg; Calcium 35mg; Fibre 1g; Sodium 6mg.

Chilli bean salsa

These beans have a pretty, speckled appearance. The smokey flavour of the chipotle chillies and the herby taste of the pasilla chilli contrast well with the tart tomatillos.

SERVES 4

130g/4¹/₂ oz/generous ¹/₂ cup pinto
   beans, soaked overnight in water
   to cover
2 chipotle chillies
1 pasilla chilli
2 garlic cloves, peeled
¹/₂ onion
200g/7oz fresh tomatillos
salt

1 Drain the beans and put them in a large pan. Pour in water to cover and place the lid on the pan. Bring to the boil, lower the heat slightly and simmer the beans for 45–50 minutes or until tender. Drain, rinse under cold water, then drain again and transfer into a bowl. Leave the beans until cold.

2 Soak the chipotle and pasilla chillies in hot water for about 10 minutes until softened. Drain, reserving the soaking water. Remove the stalks, then slit each chilli and scrape out the seeds with a small sharp knife. Chop the flesh finely and mix it to a smooth paste with a little of the soaking water.

3 Roast the garlic in a dry frying pan over medium heat until the cloves start to turn golden. Crush them and add them to the beans.

4 Chop the onion and tomatillos and stir into the beans. Add the chilli paste and mix well. Add salt to taste, cover and chill before serving.

Nutritional information per portion: Energy 97kcal/410kJ; Protein 7g; Carbohydrate 16.8g, of which sugars 3.2g; Fat 0.7g, of which saturates 0.2g; Cholesterol 0mg; Calcium 32mg; Fibre 2.9g; Sodium 10mg.

Smooth red chilli salsa

This is a very fiery salsa with an intense heat level. A dab on the plate alongside a meat or fish dish adds a fresh, clean taste, but it is not for the faint-hearted.

SERVES 12

10 fresh red chillies, roughly chopped
1 large tomato, peeled and quartered
2 garlic cloves
juice of 1 lime
60ml/4 tbsp olive oil
salt

1 Place the chillies, tomato and garlic in a food processor, then process the mixture until smooth.

2 Scrape the mixture into a small frying pan and place over medium heat. Season with salt and cook, stirring, for 10 minutes, until the sauce is thick.

3 Remove the mixture from the heat and stir in the freshly squeezed lime juice.

4 Transfer to a sterilized airtight jar and top with a thin film of olive oil before tightly screwing on the lid.

5 As long as the chilli sauce always has a film of oil on top, it will keep for weeks in the refrigerator.

Nutritional information per portion: Energy 37kcal/152kJ; Protein 0.3g; Carbohydrate 0.5g, of which sugars 0.5g; Fat 3.8g, of which saturates 0.5g; Cholesterol 0mg; Calcium 3mg; Fibre 0.1g; Sodium 2mg.

Barbecue chilli salsa

This tangy dip is very hot. The combination of finely chopped vegetables and tart vinegar dressing is the perfect partner for all types of grilled meats dishes.

SERVES 6

2 fresh green chillies
1 large tomato
1 garlic clove, crushed
1 onion, very finely chopped
15ml/1 tbsp fresh flat leaf parsley
105ml/7 tbsp olive oil
30ml/2 tbsp red wine vinegar
salt

1 Carefully slice the chillies in half and scrape out the seeds, and finely chop.

2 Peel the tomato. Scrape out the seeds and finely chop.

3 Combine the chopped chillies, crushed garlic, onion and tomato in a bowl.

4 Chop the parsley, then add to the mixture, stir well and season to taste with salt.

5 Pour in the oil and vinegar and stir well. Allow the flavours to mingle for at least 1 hour before serving with grilled meats.

Nutritional information per portion: Energy 134kcal/552kJ; Protein 0.8g; Carbohydrate 3.7g, of which sugars 2.9g; Fat 13g, of which saturates 1.8g; Cholesterol 0mg; Calcium 12mg; Fibre 0.8g; Sodium 4mg.

Hot and spicy plantain snacks

Sweet and crisp, deep-fried slices of plantain make good nibbles with drinks. Make sure the plantains are ripe – the skin should be brown and mottled – otherwise they tend to be woody rather than sweet. Be liberal with the spices as the starchy plantains can carry strong flavours.

SERVES 2–4 AS A SNACK

2 large ripe plantains
sunflower oil, for deep-frying
**1 dried red chilli, roasted, seeded
    and chopped**
15–30ml/1–2 tbsp zahtar
coarse salt

1 To peel the plantains, cut off their ends with a sharp knife and make two to three incisions in the skin from end to end, then peel off the skin. Cut the plantains into thick slices.

2 Heat the oil for deep-frying to 180°C/350°F, or until a cube of day-old bread browns in 15 seconds. Fry the plantain slices in batches until they are golden brown in colour.

3 Once a batch of plantain slices is cooked, drain them on a double layer of kitchen paper. While the plantain is still warm, place the pieces in a shallow bowl and sprinkle liberally with the dried roasted chilli, zahtar and salt.

4 Toss the ingredients thoroughly and serve immediately.

Nutritional information per portion: Energy 334kcal/1408kJ; Protein 1.9g; Carbohydrate 59.4g, of which sugars 14.4g; Fat 11.5g, of which saturates 1.3g; Cholesterol 0mg; Calcium 8mg; Fibre 2.9g; Sodium 4mg.

Chilli courgette batons

This is a spicy version of the classic Japanese tempura, using besan, or chickpea flour, in the batter. Also known as gram flour, golden besan is more commonly used in Indian cooking and gives a wonderfully crisp texture while the courgette inside becomes meltingly tender.

SERVES 4

600g/1lb 6oz courgettes (zucchini)

90g/3¹/₂oz/³/₄ cup gram flour

5ml/1 tsp baking powder

2.5ml/¹/₂ tsp turmeric

10ml/2 tsp ground coriander

5ml/1 tsp ground cumin

5ml/1 tsp chilli powder

250ml/8fl oz/1 cup beer

sunflower oil, for deep-frying

salt

steamed basmati rice, natural (plain)
    yogurt and pickles, to serve

1 Cut the courgettes into thick, finger-sized batons and set aside. Sift the gram flour, baking powder, turmeric, ground coriander, cumin and chilli powder into a large bowl. Season the mixture with salt and gradually add the beer, mixing to make a thick batter.

2 Fill a large wok one-third full with sunflower oil and heat to 180°C/ 350°F (until a cube of bread in the oil, browns in 15 seconds). Working in batches, dip each courgette baton into the spiced batter mixture and then deep-fry for 1–2 minutes, or until the batter is crisp and golden.

3 Lift the cooked batons out of the wok using a slotted spoon and place them on kitchen paper to drain. Serve the courgettes immediately while hot, accompanied by steamed basmati rice, yogurt, pickles and chutney.

Nutritional information per portion: Energy 241kcal/999kJ; Protein 7.3g; Carbohydrate 15.3g, of which sugars 4.6g; Fat 15.6g, of which saturates 1.9g; Cholesterol 0mg; Calcium 83mg; Fibre 3.8g; Sodium 15mg.

Spiced carrot and apricot rolls

These sweet, chilli carrot rolls originate from Turkey. Served with a dollop of yogurt flavoured with mint and garlic, they make a delicious snack or light lunch when served with crusty bread.

SERVES 4

8–10 carrots, cut into thick slices
2–3 slices of bread, ground
   into crumbs
4 spring onions (scallions),
   finely sliced
150g/5oz/generous ¹/₂ cup
   ready-to-eat dried apricots,
   finely chopped
45ml/3 tbsp pine nuts
1 egg
1 fresh red chilli, seeded and chopped
1 bunch of fresh dill, chopped

1 bunch of fresh basil, finely shredded
plain (all-purpose) flour, for coating
sunflower oil, for shallow-frying
salt and ground black pepper
lemon wedges, to serve

FOR THE MINT YOGURT
about 225g/8oz/1 cup thick and
   creamy natural (plain) yogurt
juice of ¹/₂ lemon
1–2 garlic cloves, crushed
1 bunch of fresh mint, finely chopped

1 Steam the carrot slices for about 25 minutes, or until very soft. While the carrots are steaming, make the mint yogurt. Beat the yogurt in a bowl with the lemon juice and garlic, season and stir in the mint. Set aside, or chill in the refrigerator.

2 Mash the carrots to a paste. Add the breadcrumbs, spring onions, apricots and pine nuts and mix together well. Beat in the egg and stir in the chilli and herbs. Season with salt and pepper.

3 Place a small heap of flour on to a flat surface. Take a plum-sized portion of the carrot mixture in your fingers and mould it into a small oblong roll. Coat the carrot roll in the flour and transfer it to a large plate. Repeat with the rest of the mixture, to make 12 to16 rolls.

4 Heat the oil in a frying pan. Fry the carrot rolls for about 8–10 minutes, turning them occasionally, until golden brown. Drain and serve hot, with lemon wedges and the mint yogurt.

Nutritional information per portion: Energy 401kcal/1673kJ; Protein 8.7g; Carbohydrate 46g, of which sugars 29.1g; Fat 21.5g, of which saturates 2.5g; Cholesterol 48mg; Calcium 144mg; Fibre 8.5g; Sodium 145mg.

Stuffed chillies

This dish, also known as chillies rellenos, are popular all over Mexico. The type of chilli used differs from region to region, but larger chillies are obviously easier to stuff than smaller ones.

MAKES 6

6 fresh poblano or Anaheim chillies
2 potatoes, total weight about
    400g/14oz
200g/7oz/scant 1 cup cream cheese
200g/7oz/1¾ cups grated mature
    (sharp) Cheddar cheese
5ml/1 tsp salt

2.5ml/½ tsp ground black pepper
2 eggs, separated
115g/4oz/1 cup plain (all-purpose) flour
2.5ml/½ tsp white pepper
oil, for deep-frying
chilli flakes, to garnish (optional)

1 Make a slit down one side of each chilli. Place in a dry frying pan over medium heat, turning frequently until the skins blister. Place in a plastic bag and set aside for 20 minutes. Peel off the skins and remove the seeds through the slits. Dry with kitchen paper and set aside.

2 Scrub or peel the potatoes and cut into 1cm/½in dice. Bring a large pan of water to the boil, add the potatoes and simmer for 5 minutes or until the potatoes are just tender. Do not overcook. Drain them thoroughly.

3 Put the cream cheese in a bowl and stir in the grated cheese, with 2.5ml/½ tsp of the salt and the black pepper. Add the potato and mix gently. Spoon some of the potato filling into each chilli. Put on a plate, cover with clear film (plastic wrap) and chill for 1 hour.

4 Put the egg whites in a clean, grease-free bowl and whisk them to firm peaks. In a separate bowl, beat the yolks until pale, then fold in the whites. Scrape the mixture on to a shallow dish. Spread out the flour in another shallow dish and season it with the remaining salt and the white pepper.

5 Heat the oil for deep-frying to 190°C/375°F. Coat a few chillies first in flour and then in egg before adding carefully to the hot oil. Fry the chillies in batches until golden and crisp. Drain on kitchen paper and serve hot, garnished with a sprinkle of chilli flakes for extra heat, if desired.

Nutritional information per portion: Energy 605kcal/2512kJ; Protein 18.5g; Carbohydrate 30.8g, of which sugars 1.9g; Fat 45.4g, of which saturates 27.7g; Cholesterol 159mg; Calcium 385mg; Fibre 1.5g; Sodium 478mg.

Aubergines in a chilli sauce

This fiery dish is a great Indonesian favourite, both in the home and at the street stall. You can make it with large aubergines, cut in half and baked, or with small ones, butterflied.

SERVES 4

2 large aubergines (eggplants), cut in half lengthways, or 4 small auberines, butterflied
45–60ml/3–4 tbsp coconut oil
4 shallots, finely chopped
4 garlic cloves, finely chopped
25g/1oz fresh root ginger, finely chopped
3–4 red chillies, seeded and finely chopped
400g/14oz can tomatoes, drained
5–10ml/1–2 tsp palm sugar (jaggery)
juice of 2 limes
salt
1 small bunch fresh coriander (cilantro), to garnish

1 Preheat the oven to 180°C/350°F/Gas 4. Put the aubergines on a baking tray and brush with 30ml/2 tbsp of the coconut oil. Bake in the oven for 40 minutes, until they are soft.

2 Using a mortar and pestle, or a food processor or blender, grind or process the shallots, garlic, ginger and chillies to a smooth paste.

3 Heat the remaining 15ml/1 tbsp of oil in a frying pan, stir in the spice paste and cook for 1–2 minutes.

4 Add the tomatoes and sugar and cook for a further 3–4 minutes, until heated, then stir in the lime juice and a little salt to taste.

5 Put the baked aubergines in a serving dish and gently press down the flesh using the back of a spoon to create a small hollow. Fill this with the sauce and spoon more of the sauce over the aubergines.

6 Garnish the aubergines with the coriander and serve immediately.

Nutritional information per portion: Energy 100kcal/419kJ; Protein 2.1g; Carbohydrate 9.4g, of which sugars 8.8g; Fat 6.4g, of which saturates 0.9g; Cholesterol 0mg; Calcium 42mg; Fibre 3.7g; Sodium 15mg.

Chilli pakoras

These red-hot potato bites are popular fried snacks found across South-east Asia. They taste delicious when served alongside a fragrant and fruity chutney dipping sauce.

MAKES 25

15ml/1 tbsp sunflower oil
20ml/4 tsp cumin seeds
5ml/1 tsp black mustard seeds
1 small onion, finely chopped
10ml/2 tsp grated fresh root ginger
2 green chillies, seeded and chopped
600g/1lb 6oz potatoes, cooked
200g/7oz fresh peas
juice of 1 lemon
90ml/6 tbsp chopped fresh coriander (cilantro) leaves
115g/4oz/1 cup gram flour
25g/1oz/¼ cup self-raising (self-rising) flour
40g/1½oz/⅓ cup rice flour
large pinch of turmeric
10ml/2 tsp crushed coriander seeds
350ml/12fl oz/1½ cups water
vegetable oil, for deep-frying
salt and ground black pepper

1 Heat a wok or large frying pan over medium heat and add the sunflower oil. When the oil is hot, fry the cumin and mustard seeds for 1–2 minutes.

2 Add the onion, ginger and green chillies to the wok and cook for a further 3–4 minutes. Add the cooked potatoes and peas and stir-fry for 5–6 minutes. Season, then stir in the lemon juice and coriander leaves.

3 Divide into 25 portions, roughly shaping each portion into a ball, then leave to chill in the refrigerator.

4 To make the batter, put the gram flour, self-raising flour and rice flour in a bowl. Season and add the turmeric and coriander seeds. Gradually whisk in the water to make a smooth batter.

5 Fill a wok one-third full of oil and heat to 180°C/350°F. Working in batches, dip the chilled balls in the batter, then drop them into the oil and deep-fry for 1–2 minutes, or until golden.

6 Drain the cooked balls on kitchen paper, and serve immediately while hot.

Nutritional information per portion: Energy 126kcal/525kJ; Protein 4.1g; Carbohydrate 8.3g, of which sugars 2.6g; Fat 8.8g, of which saturates 5.2g; Cholesterol 0mg; Calcium 35mg; Fibre 1.3g; Sodium 16mg.

Tofu, pumpkin and chilli rolls

These spicy rolls are one of the best Vietnamese 'do-it-yourself' dishes. You place all the ingredients on the table with the rice wrappers for everyone to assemble their own rolls.

SERVES 4–5

about 30ml/2 tbsp groundnut (peanut)
   or sesame oil
175g/6oz tofu, rinsed and
   patted dry
4 shallots, halved and sliced
2 garlic cloves, finely chopped
350g/12oz pumpkin flesh, cut into strips
1 carrot, cut into strips
15ml/1 tbsp soy sauce
3–4 green Thai chillies, seeded and
   finely sliced

1 crispy lettuce, torn into strips
1 bunch fresh basil, stalks removed
115g/4oz/²/₃ cup roasted
   peanuts, chopped
100ml/3¹/₂fl oz/scant ¹/₂ cup
   hoisin sauce
20 dried rice wrappers
salt
chilli sauce (optional), to serve

1 Heat a heavy pan and smear with oil. Place the tofu in the pan and sear on both sides. Transfer to a plate and cut into thin strips.

2 Heat 30ml/2 tbsp oil in the pan and stir in the shallots and garlic. Add the pumpkin and carrot, then pour in the soy sauce and 120ml/4fl oz/¹/₂ cup water. Add a little salt and cook gently until the vegetables have softened but still have a bite to them.

3 Meanwhile, arrange the tofu, chillies, lettuce, basil, peanuts and hoisin sauce in separate dishes and put them on the table. Fill a bowl with hot water and place it on the table or fill a small bowl for each person, and place the wrappers beside it. Transfer the vegetable mixture to a dish and place on the table.

4 To eat, dip a wrapper in the water for a few seconds to soften. Lay it flat on the table or on a plate and, just off-centre, spread a few strips of lettuce, then the pumpkin mixture, some tofu, a sprinkling of chillies, some hoisin sauce, some basil leaves and peanuts, to layer the ingredients. Pull the shorter edge (the side with filling on it) over the stack, tuck in the sides and roll into a cylinder. Dip the roll into chilli sauce, if you like.

Nutritional information per portion: Energy 402kcal/1669kJ; Protein 14g; Carbohydrate 29g, of which sugars 13g; Fat 26g, of which saturates 5g; Cholesterol 0mg; Calcium 321mg; Fibre 4.1g; Sodium 0.4g.

Tofu stuffed with chilli

An easy accompaniment for a main course, or a great lunch. Squares of fried tofu stuffed with a blend of chilli and chestnut give a piquant jolt to the delicate flavour of the tofu.

SERVES 2

2 blocks firm tofu
30ml/2 tbsp Thai fish sauce
5ml/1 tsp sesame oil
2 eggs
7.5ml/1¹/₂ tsp cornflour (cornstarch)
vegetable oil, for shallow-frying

FOR THE FILLING

2 green chillies, finely chopped
2 chestnuts, finely chopped
6 garlic cloves, crushed
10ml/2 tsp sesame seeds

1 Cut the blocks of tofu into 2cm/³/₄in slices, and then cut each slice in half. Place the tofu slices on a piece of kitchen paper to absorb any excess water.

2 Mix together the Thai fish sauce and sesame oil. Transfer the tofu slices to a plate and coat them evenly with the fish sauce mixture. Leave to marinate for 20 minutes.

3 Meanwhile, put all the filling ingredients into a large bowl and combine them together thoroughly. Put to one side until needed.

4 Beat the eggs in a dish. Add the cornflour and whisk until well combined. Take the slices of tofu and dip them into the beaten egg mixture, ensuring an even coating on all sides.

5 Place a frying pan over medium heat and add the vegetable oil. Add the tofu slices to the pan and fry, turning once, until golden.

6 Once cooked, make a slit down the middle of each slice with a sharp knife, without cutting all the way through. Gently push a large pinch of the filling into each slice, and serve.

Nutritional information per portion: Energy 291kcal/1213kJ; Protein 23g; Carbohydrate 7.8g, of which sugars 1.3g; Fat 19.1g, of which saturates 3.4g; Cholesterol 209mg; Calcium 1014mg; Fibre 0.8g; Sodium 88mg.

Deep-fried eggs with red chillies

Also known as mother-in-law eggs in China, this spicy deep-fried egg dish is full of delicious flavours, the combination of red-hot chilli and the tangy tamarind is simply divine.

SERVES 4–6

30ml/2 tbsp vegetable oil
6 shallots, thinly sliced
6 garlic cloves, thinly sliced
6 fresh red chillies, sliced
oil, for deep-frying
6 hard-boiled eggs, shelled
sprigs of fresh coriander (cilantro),
    to garnish
salad leaves, to serve

FOR THE SAUCE

75g/3oz/6 tbsp palm sugar (jaggery) or
    light muscovado (brown) sugar
75ml/5 tbsp Thai fish sauce
90ml/6 tbsp tamarind juice

1 Make the sauce. Put the palm or muscovado sugar, Thai fish sauce and tamarind juice into a pan.

2 Bring to the boil, stirring until the sugar dissolves, lower the heat and simmer for 5 minutes. Taste and add more sugar, fish sauce or tamarind juice, if needed. Transfer to a bowl.

3 Heat the vegetable oil in a frying pan and cook the shallots, garlic and chillies for 5 minutes. Transfer to a bowl and set aside.

4 Heat the oil in a wok to 190°C/375°F or until a cube of bread, added to the oil, browns in about 45 seconds. Deep-fry the eggs for about 3–5 minutes, or until golden. Remove from the oil and drain well on kitchen paper.

5 Cut the eggs into quarters and arrange them on a bed of salad leaves. Drizzle with the prepared sauce and sprinkle over the shallot mixture. Garnish with the coriander sprigs and serve immediately.

Nutritional information per portion: Energy 215kcal/894kJ; Protein 14.2g; Carbohydrate 2.4g, of which sugars 2.2g; Fat 16.9g, of which saturates 4.2g; Cholesterol 381mg; Calcium 112mg; Fibre 0.8g; Sodium 1223mg.

Chilli cheese potatoes

This Peruvian dish of sliced potatoes, eggs and boiled corn on the cob makes a wonderful and substantial snack or light lunch, especially when it is served with the red-hot chilli sauce.

SERVES 6

1kg/2¼lb floury potatoes
2 corn on the cob
a few kalamata olives
3 hard-boiled eggs, halved
6–12 lettuce leaves
salt
red chilli, cut into fine strips,
    to garnish (optional)

FOR THE SAUCE

500g/1¼lb queso fresco or mild
    feta cheese
3 red chillies, seeded
juice of 1 lime
3 crackers
45ml/3 tbsp vegetable oil
120ml/4fl oz/½ cup milk

1 Put the potatoes in lightly salted water and boil for 15–20 minutes, until just tender. Meanwhile, put all the ingredients for the sauce into a blender or food processor and blend until smooth, adding salt or chilli to taste.

2 When the potatoes are cooked, drain them and allow to cool a little, then peel while they are still warm and slice thickly.

3 Fill a large pan with unsalted water. Boil the corn on the cob for about 10 minutes, then drain and cut into chunks.

4 To assemble the dish, lay one or two lettuce leaves on each plate and arrange potato slices on top, and cover with sauce.

5 Add the olives, eggs and corn to the plate. Garnish with red chilli strips.

Nutritional information per portion: Energy 445kcal/1860kJ; Protein 21.2g; Carbohydrate 32.2g, of which sugars 5g; Fat 26.6g, of which saturates 13.1g; Cholesterol 155mg; Calcium 357mg; Fibre 2.3g; Sodium 1666mg.

Spicy potato with tuna

These delightful little snacks, made with chilli sauce, are simple to make and very tasty. You can garnish it with olives and slices of egg and extra strips of red chilli if you wish.

SERVES 4

500g/1¼lb King Edward potatoes
juice of 1 lime
30ml/2 tbsp chilli sauce
30ml/2 tbsp vegetable oil
5ml/1 tsp salt
lettuce leaves
4 kalamata olives
2 hard-boiled eggs, sliced
salt and ground black pepper
red chilli, cut into fine strips, to
    garnish (optional)

FOR THE FILLING

200g/7oz can tuna fish in brine
150ml/¼pint/⅔ cup mayonnaise

1 Boil the whole potatoes in lightly salted water for 20 minutes, until tender, then drain. When cool enough to handle, peel and mash to a smooth purée. Place the mashed potato in a bowl, cover and leave to cool.

2 Meanwhile, to make the filling, drain the tuna fish thoroughly, place it in a bowl and mix with the mayonnaise. Cover and set aside.

3 When the potato is cold add the lime juice, chilli sauce, oil and salt, and beat the mixture until it is even in colour and flavour. Season.

4 Line a plate with lettuce leaves, then spread half the potato mixture over the lettuce. Spoon the tuna filling on top evenly, then spread the remaining potato over the top. Garnish with the eggs, olives and the chilli strips. Serve.

Nutritional information per portion: Energy 490kcal/2038kJ; Protein 17.6g; Carbohydrate 22.6g, of which sugars 3.8g; Fat 37.3g, of which saturates 5.7g; Cholesterol 149mg; Calcium 31mg; Fibre 1.3g; Sodium 462mg.

Seafood pancake with mixed chillies

These little bites combine the silky texture of squid and scallops with the crunch and piquancy of spring onions. They makes a delicious snack, especially when served with the spicy dipping sauce.

SERVES 4

90g/3½oz squid, trimmed, cleaned,
   skinned and sliced
2 oysters, removed from the shell
5 clams, removed from the shell
5 small prawns (shrimp), shelled
3 scallops, removed from the shell
15ml/1 tbsp vegetable oil
5 spring onions (scallions), sliced into
   thin strips
½ red chilli, seeded and cut into
   thin strips
½ green chilli, seeded and cut into
   thin strips
50g/2oz enoki mushrooms
1 garlic clove, thinly sliced
salt and ground black pepper

FOR THE BATTER

115g/4oz/1 cup plain (all-purpose) flour
40g/1½oz/⅓ cup cornflour
   (cornstarch)
2 eggs, beaten
5ml/1 tsp salt
5ml/1 tsp sugar

FOR THE DIPPING SAUCE

90ml/6 tbsp light soy sauce
22.5ml/4½ tsp rice vinegar
1 spring onion (scallion), shredded
1 red chilli, finely shredded
1 garlic clove, crushed
5ml/1 tsp sesame oil
5ml/1 tsp sesame seeds

1 For the batter, sift the flour into a large bowl. Add the rest of the batter ingredients with 200ml/7fl oz/scant 1 cup iced water and whisk until smooth. Set aside. Put the seafood into another large bowl. Season, and leave to stand for 10 minutes.

2 Meanwhile, make the dipping sauce. Put all the ingredients in a small bowl, mixing well until combined.

3 Heat the vegetable oil in a large frying pan. Pour one-third of the batter in, spreading it evenly in the pan. Place the spring onions, chillies, mushrooms and garlic on to the pancake and then add the seafood.

4 Pour over the remaining batter and cook, turning once, until the pancake is golden brown on both sides. Slice the pancake into bitesize pieces and serve on a large plate with the dipping sauce.

Nutritional information per portion: Energy 255kcal/1077kJ; Protein 16.5g; Carbohydrate 33.7g, of which sugars 1.9g; Fat 7.1g, of which saturates 1.4g; Cholesterol 232mg; Calcium 80mg; Fibre 1.4g; Sodium 613mg.

Fried whitebait in spicy dressing

Serve these tangy morsels as an appetizer with drinks or as a main course with a salad of cold mashed potatoes dressed with onions, jalapeño chillies, olive oil and lemon juice.

SERVES 4

800g/1³/₄lb whitebait or tiny white fish
juice of 2 lemons
5ml/1 tsp salt
plain (all-purpose) flour, for dusting
vegetable oil, for frying
2 onions, chopped or thinly sliced
2.5–5ml/¹/₂–1 tsp cumin seeds
2 carrots, thinly sliced
2 jalapeño chillies, chopped
8 garlic cloves, roughly chopped
120ml/4fl oz/¹/₂ cup white wine vinegar
2–3 large pinches of dried oregano
15–30ml/1–2 tbsp chopped fresh
  coriander (cilantro) leaves
slices of corn on the cob, black olives and
  coriander (cilantro), to serve

1 Put the whitebait in a bowl, add the lemon juice and salt and leave for 30–60 minutes. Then remove the fish and dust with plain flour.

2 Heat the vegetable oil in a deep-frying pan until the oil is hot enough to turn a cube of bread golden brown in 30 seconds. Fry the fish in small batches, until crisp, then place on to a plate and set aside.

3 In a separate pan, heat 30ml/2 tbsp of oil. Add the onions, cumin seeds, carrots, chillies and garlic and fry for 5 minutes. Stir in the vinegar, oregano and coriander and cook for 1–2 minutes. Pour the onion mixture over the fried fish and leave to cool.

4 Serve the fish at room temperature, with slices of corn on the cob, black olives and chopped coriander leaves.

Nutritional information per portion: Energy 1087kcal/4504kJ; Protein 40.3g; Carbohydrate 18.5g, of which sugars 5.9g; Fat 95.3g, of which saturates 8.9g; Cholesterol 0mg; Calcium 1734mg; Fibre 2.3g; Sodium 471mg.

Spicy scallops with mushrooms and egg

Fragrant steamed scallops served in their shells are given a spicy twist with shreds of chilli pepper. Tiny enoki mushrooms and strips of sautéed egg yolk match the elegant flavours of the seafood, and lemon rind and shredded seaweed make an attractive garnish.

SERVES 2

5 scallops, with shells
30ml/2 tbsp vegetable oil
10ml/2 tsp sesame oil
2 egg yolks, beaten
1 red chilli, seeded and finely sliced
1/2 green (bell) pepper, finely sliced
65g/2¹/₂oz enoki mushrooms
salt and ground white pepper
1 sheet dried seaweed, sliced into
   thin strips, grated rind of 1 lemon,
   to garnish

1 Scrub the scallop shells. Carefully remove the scallops from the shells, then remove the membrane and hard white muscle from each one.

2 Heat 15ml/1 tbsp vegetable oil in a wok and stir-fry the scallops until browned. Season with sesame oil, salt and pepper. Clean the scallop shells in hot water. Add 10ml/2 tsp oil to the wok and heat over low heat. Pour in the egg yolks and add a pinch of salt. Cook to form a thin omelette. Once the omelette is set, slice into strips.

3 Add the chilli and pepper to the pan, adding oil if required, and stir-fry with for 3–4 minutes. Place the scallop shells in a steamer, and set one scallop on each shell. Place the pepper mixture, some omelette strips and some mushrooms on each shell, and steam for 4 minutes. Garnish with the seaweed and a sprinkling of the lemon rind, and serve.

Nutritional information per portion: Energy 325kcal/1356kJ; Protein 27.2g; Carbohydrate 6.8g, of which sugars 3.1g; Fat 21.3g, of which saturates 3.8g; Cholesterol 249mg; Calcium 59mg; Fibre 1.2g; Sodium 193mg.

Steamed chilli scallops

Serve these juicy, fragrant scallops with the subtle chilli spices as an indulgent main course for a special occasion. For the best results, use the freshest scallops you can find.

SERVES 4

24 king scallops in their shells, cleaned
15ml/1 tbsp very finely shredded fresh root ginger
5ml/1 tsp very finely chopped garlic
1 large red chilli, seeded and very finely chopped
15ml/1 tbsp light soy sauce
15ml/1 tbsp Chinese rice wine
a few drops of sesame oil
2–3 spring onions (scallions), very finely shredded
15ml/1 tbsp very finely chopped fresh chives
noodles or rice, to serve

1 Carefully remove the scallops from their shells, then remove the membrane and hard white muscle from each one.

2 Have two large plates to hand that are small enough to fit inside a wok. Arrange the scallops on to the two plates. Rinse the shells, dry them and set aside.

3 Fill two woks with 5cm/2in water and place a trivet in the base of each one. Bring to the boil.

4 Put the ginger, garlic, chilli, soy sauce, rice wine, sesame oil, spring onions and chives in a bowl and mix together. Spoon the mixture over the scallops.

5 Lower a plate of scallops into each of the woks. Turn the heat to low, cover and steam for 10–12 minutes, or until just cooked through.

6 Divide the scallops among four, or eight, of the reserved shells and serve immediately.

Nutritional information per portion: Energy 392kcal/1621kJ; Protein 13.6g; Carbohydrate 4.5g, of which sugars 2.5g; Fat 34.1g, of which saturates 22.4g; Cholesterol 115mg; Calcium 63mg; Fibre 0.4g; Sodium 168mg.

Chilli prawn skewers

Try to get the freshest prawns you can for this recipe. If you buy whole prawns, you will need to remove the heads and shells, leaving the tail section intact. Serve with extra lime wedges.

SERVES 4

16 giant raw prawns (shrimp), shelled with the tail section left intact
1 lime, cut into 8 wedges
60ml/4 tbsp sweet chilli sauce

1 Place eight bamboo skewers in a bowl of cold water and leave to soak for at least 10 minutes, then preheat the grill (broiler) to high.

2 Thread a prawn on to each skewer, then a lime wedge, then another prawn until you have four prawns on each skewer.

3 Arrange the skewers on a baking sheet and brush the sweet chilli sauce over the prawns and lime wedges. Grill (broil) for about 2 minutes, turning them once, until cooked through.

4 Serve immediately with extra chilli sauce for dipping.

Nutritional information per portion: Energy 59kcal/247kJ; Protein 11.3g; Carbohydrate 2.6g, of which sugars 2.5g; Fat 0.4g, of which saturates 0.1g; Cholesterol 122mg; Calcium 61mg; Fibre 0.1g; Sodium 242mg.

Chilli seafood satay

One of the tastiest satay recipes, this shrimp and scallop dish is succulent, spicy and extremely moreish. Serve with lime wedges or with rice and a fruity salad if you wish.

SERVES 4

250g/9oz shelled shrimp or prawns, deveined and chopped
250g/9oz shelled scallops, chopped
30ml/2 tbsp potato, tapioca or rice flour
5ml/1 tsp baking powder
12–16 wooden, metal, lemon grass or sugar cane skewers
1 lime, quartered, to serve

FOR THE SPICE PASTE
2 shallots, chopped
2 garlic cloves, chopped
2–3 red chillies, seeded and chopped

25g/1oz galangal or fresh root ginger, chopped
15g/1/2oz fresh turmeric, chopped or 2.5ml/1/2 tsp ground turmeric
2–3 lemon grass stalks, chopped
15–30ml/1–2 tbsp palm or groundnut (peanut) oil
5ml/1 tsp shrimp paste
15ml/1 tbsp tamarind paste
5ml/1 tsp palm sugar (jaggery)

1 Make the paste. In a mortar and pestle, pound the shallots, garlic, chillies, galangal, turmeric and lemon grass to form a paste.

2 Heat the oil in a wok or heavy frying pan, stir in the paste. Fry until fragrant. Add the shrimp paste, tamarind and sugar and cook, stirring, until the mixture darkens. Set aside to cool.

3 In a bowl, pound the shrimps and scallops together to form a paste, or blend them in an electric blender or food processor. Beat in the spice paste, then the flour and baking powder, and beat until blended. Chill in the refrigerator for 1 hour. If using wooden skewers, soak them in water for about 30 minutes.

4 Using your fingers, scoop up lumps of the shellfish paste and wrap it around the skewers. Place each skewer under a medium grill (broiler) and cook for 3 minutes on each side, until golden brown. Serve with the lime wedges to squeeze over them.

Nutritional information per portion: Energy 220kcal/922kJ; Protein 27.1g; Carbohydrate 11.5g, of which sugars 1g; Fat 7.3g, of which saturates 1g; Cholesterol 151mg; Calcium 99mg; Fibre 1.5g; Sodium 249mg.

Chilli-stuffed squid

Squid stuffed with tangy chilli mixture are quickly cooked under a hot grill. The tentacles are a wonderfully tasty part of the squid so thread them on to the skewers as well.

SERVES 6

12 whole baby squid, total weight about 675g/1¹/₂lb, cleaned
45ml/3 tbsp extra virgin olive oil, plus extra for coating
2 onions, finely chopped
3 garlic cloves, crushed
25g/1oz/2 tbsp walnuts, finely chopped
7.5ml/1¹/₂ tsp ground sumac or squeeze of lemon juice
1.5ml/¹/₄ tsp finely chopped fresh chilli or dried chilli flakes
75–90g/3–3¹/₂oz rocket (arugula), any tough stalks removed
115g/4oz/1 cup cooked rice
salt and ground black pepper
lemon and lime wedges, to serve

1 Prepare the squid, washing the clumps of tentacles and body well, inside and out, under cold running water. Put the tentacles on a plate, cover and chill. Pull the side flaps or wings away from the body, chop them finely and set aside. Reserve the squid body with the tentacles.

2 Heat a frying pan. Add the oil, onions and garlic and fry for 5 minutes, or until the onions are soft and golden. Add the chopped squid wings and fry for 1 minute, then stir in the walnuts, sumac and chilli. Add the rocket and stir-fry until wilted. Stir in the rice, season well and tip into a bowl to cool.

3 Stuff each squid with the cool mixture and thread two on to each skewer, with two tentacles. Toss in oil and salt. Cook under a medium grill (broiler) for about 1¹/₂ minutes on each side. When the stuffed squid is golden in colour, move to a cooler part of the grill to cook for 1¹/₂ minutes more on each side. Serve with lemon and lime wedges.

Nutritional information per portion: Energy 356kcal/1487kJ; Protein 21.8g; Carbohydrate 15.2g, of which sugars 3.6g; Fat 23.6g, of which saturates 11.1g; Cholesterol 321mg; Calcium 55mg;

Chilli crab cakes

Crab meat makes wonderful fish cakes and combines well with chilli, as shown by these gutsy morsels. They make great snacks and are also the perfect choice for parties.

MAKES ABOUT 15

225g/8oz white crab meat
   (fresh, frozen or canned)
115g/4oz cooked floury
   potatoes, mashed
30ml/2 tbsp fresh herb seasoning
2.5ml/1/2 tsp mild mustard
2.5ml/1/2 tsp ground black pepper
1/2 fresh hot chilli, finely chopped
5ml/1 tsp fresh oregano
1 egg, beaten
plain (all-purpose) flour, for dredging
vegetable oil, for frying
lime wedges and coriander (cilantro)
   sprigs, to garnish
fresh whole chilli peppers, to serve

1 Put the crab meat, potatoes, herb seasoning, mustard, pepper and chilli, oregano and egg in a large bowl and mix together well.

2 Chill the crab mixture for at least 30 minutes. Shape the chilled crab mixture into small rounds and dredge with flour, brushing and shaking off any excess.

3 Heat a little vegetable oil in a frying pan and fry, a few cakes at a time, for 2–3 minutes on each side. Drain the cooked cakes on kitchen paper and keep them warm in a low-heated oven while cooking the remainder. Garnish with lime wedges and coriander sprigs, and serve with whole chillies.

Nutritional information per portion: Energy 190kcal/795kJ; Protein 16.2g; Carbohydrate 7.1g, of which sugars 0.6g; Fat 11g, of which saturates 1.4g; Cholesterol 55mg; Calcium 35mg; Fibre 0.3g; Sodium 388mg.

Mussels in a chilli sauce

This is a popular dish in Peru. The evaporated milk adds a sweetness, while plenty of hot chilli sauce gives it heat. Use large frozen mussels if you can't find fresh ones.

SERVES 6

1kg/2¼lb New Zealand greenshell
   mussels, fresh or frozen
100g/3¾oz shelled walnuts
350ml/12fl oz/1½ cups evaporated milk
12 slices white bread, reduced
   to crumbs
75ml/5 tbsp vegetable oil
1 large red onion, finely chopped

4 garlic cloves, crushed
45ml/3 tbsp chilli sauce
5ml/1 tsp ground turmeric
2.5ml/½ tsp ground black pepper
15ml/1 tbsp chopped parsley, to garnish
1 hard-boiled egg, sliced, to garnish
rice and peas or boiled potatoes,
   to serve

1 If using fresh whole mussels, scrub them, and remove the beards. Discard any that are open and fail to close when tapped sharply. Place the mussels in a large pan with 2 litres/3½ pints/ 8 cups water. Bring to the boil then reduce the heat and simmer for 20 minutes. Drain, reserving the stock, and discarding any mussels that do not open.

2 Remove all but 12 mussels from their shells, and keep warm. Do the same if using frozen mussels. At this point some Peruvian cooks would remove the dark part with a teaspoon.

3 Put the walnuts in a blender or food processor with a little of the evaporated milk and grind to a purée. Soak the breadcrumbs in the rest of the milk for 15 minutes.

4 Heat the oil in a large pan and fry the onion and garlic for 10 minutes, until caramelized. Add the chilli sauce, turmeric and pepper. Add the bread and milk mixture and 500ml/17fl oz/generous 2 cups of the reserved stock to the pan. Simmer for 10 minutes, stirring constantly to avoid the mixture sticking to the base of the pan. Stir in the shelled mussels and the puréed walnuts and simmer for 5 minutes.

5 Turn the mixture into a serving dish and garnish with the mussels in their shells, chopped parsley and hard-boiled egg. Serve accompanied by rice and peas or boiled potatoes.

Nutritional information per portion: Energy 437kcal/1831kJ; Protein 20.7g; Carbohydrate 34.3g, of which sugars 8.5g; Fat 25.2g, of which saturates 3.8g; Cholesterol 30mg; Calcium 331mg; Fibre 1.5g; Sodium 455mg.

Chilli chicken livers

Sautéed offal, such as liver and kidney, makes a tasty appetizer. This dish of chicken livers is delicious and tangy and the cumin and dried chilli will set your taste buds alight.

SERVES 4

30–45ml/2–3 tbsp olive oil

2–3 garlic cloves, chopped

1 dried red chilli, chopped

5ml/1 tsp cumin seeds

450g/1lb chicken livers, trimmed and cut into bitesize chunks

5ml/1 tsp ground coriander

handful of roasted hazelnuts, chopped

10–15ml/2–3 tsp orange flower water

1/2 preserved lemon, finely sliced

salt and ground black pepper

small bunch of fresh coriander (cilantro), finely chopped, to garnish

1 Heat the olive oil in a heavy frying pan and stir in the garlic, chilli and cumin seeds.

2 Add the chicken livers and toss over the heat until they are browned on all sides. Reduce the heat a little and continue to cook for 3–5 minutes.

3 When the livers are almost cooked, add the ground coriander and hazelnuts. Stir in the orange flower water and preserved lemon. Season to taste with salt and pepper.

4 Serve immediately, sprinkled with a little fresh coriander.

Nutritional information per portion: Energy 242kcal/1006kJ; Protein 22.2g; Carbohydrate 1.5g, of which sugars 0.8g; Fat 16.4g, of which saturates 2.2g; Cholesterol 428mg; Calcium 54mg; Fibre 1.5g; Sodium 91mg.

Chinese chilli chicken wings

Lemon is frequently used for marinades in Chinese cuisine. Here the lemon combines with ginger, chilli and garlic to give roasted chicken wings an exotic and spicy flavour.

SERVES 4

12 chicken wings
3 garlic cloves, crushed
4cm/1¹/₂in piece fresh root ginger, peeled and grated
juice of 1 large lemon
45ml/3 tbsp soy sauce
45ml/3 tbsp clear honey
2.5ml/¹/₂ tsp chilli powder
150ml/¹/₄ pint/²/₃ cup chicken stock
salt and ground black pepper
lemon and lime wedges, to serve

1 Remove the wing tips (pinions) and discard. Cut the wings into two pieces. Put the chicken pieces into a shallow dish, cover and set aside.

2 Mix together the garlic, ginger, lemon and soy sauce in a small jug (pitcher). Blend in the honey, chilli powder, seasoning and chicken stock. Pour the mixture over the chicken wings and turn to coat completely. Cover and marinate in the refrigerator overnight.

3 Preheat the oven to 220°C/425°F/ Gas 7. Remove the chicken wings from the marinade and arrange them in a roasting pan. Roast for about 25 minutes, basting at least twice with the marinade during cooking.

4 Place the wings on a serving plate. Add the remaining marinade to the roasting pan and bring to the boil until it thickens. Spoon a little on to the wings. Serve immediately, with the lemon and lime wedges.

Nutritional information per portion: Energy 585kcal/2446kJ; Protein 35.4g; Carbohydrate 43.5g, of which sugars 7.2g; Fat 31.2g, of which saturates 4.5g; Cholesterol 292mg; Calcium 170mg; Fibre 5.1g; Sodium 744mg.

Pork and chilli crêpes

French in style, but Vietnamese in flavour, these delightfully crisp and sizzling crêpes, made with coconut milk and filled with prawns, chillies, mushrooms and beansprouts are out of this world.

SERVES 4

115g/4oz/^{1}/$_2$ cup minced (ground) pork
15ml/1 tbsp nuoc mam
2 garlic cloves, crushed
175g/6oz/^{2}/$_3$ cup button (white)
   mushrooms, finely sliced
about 60ml/4 tbsp vegetable oil
1–2 green or red Thai chillies
115g/4oz prawns (shrimp)
1 onion, finely sliced
225g/8oz/1 cup beansprouts
1 small bunch fresh coriander (cilantro)
salt and ground black pepper

FOR THE BATTER

115g/4oz/1 cup rice flour
10ml/2 tsp ground turmeric
10ml/2 tsp curry powder
5ml/1 tsp sugar
2.5ml/^{1}/$_2$ tsp salt
300ml/^{1}/$_2$ pint/1^1/$_4$ cups canned
   coconut milk
4 spring onions (scallions)

1 To make the batter, beat the rice flour, spices, sugar and salt with the coconut milk and 300ml/^{1}/$_2$ pint/1^1/$_4$ cups water, until smooth. Trim and slice the spring onions and stir into the batter. Leave to stand for 30 minutes.

2 In a bowl, mix the pork with the nuoc mam, garlic and seasoning. Lightly sauté the sliced mushrooms in 15ml/1 tbsp of the oil and set aside. Slice the chillies in half scrape out the seeds, then finely slice. Then, wash the prawns in cold water and remove the shells and veins.

3 Heat 10ml/2 tsp of the oil in a non-stick pan. Stir in a quarter of the onion and the chillies, then add a quarter each of the pork and the prawns. Pour in 150ml/^{1}/$_4$ pint/^{2}/$_3$ cup of the batter, swirling the pan so that it covers the pork and prawns.

4 Pile a quarter of the beansprouts and mushrooms on one side of the crêpe. Reduce the heat and cover the pan for 2–3 minutes. Cook the crêpe for another 2 minutes until brown underneath. Chop the coriander leaves and sprinkle over the filling and fold the crêpe. Remove the crêpe from the heat and keep warm while you make the remaining crêpes.

Nutritional information per portion: Energy 379kcal/1581kJ; Protein 18g; Carbohydrate 37g, of which sugars 9g; Fat 18g, of which saturates 3g; Cholesterol 77mg; Calcium 119mg; Fibre 3.2g; Sodium 50mg.

Chilli-spiced beef and potato Puffs

These pillows of pastry filled with beef, chilli and potatoes are served straight from the wok. The light pastry puffs up in the hot oil and contrasts enticingly with the fiery beef.

SERVES 4

15ml/1 tbsp sunflower oil

1/2 small onion, finely chopped

3 garlic cloves, crushed

5ml/1 tsp fresh root ginger, grated

1 red chilli, seeded and chopped

30ml/2 tbsp hot curry powder

75g/3oz minced (ground) beef

115g/4oz mashed potato

60ml/4 tbsp chopped fresh coriander (cilantro)

2 sheets ready-rolled, fresh puff pastry

1 egg, lightly beaten

vegetable oil, for deep-frying

salt and ground black pepper

fresh coriander (cilantro) leaves, to garnish

tomato ketchup, to serve

1 Heat the oil in a wok, then add the onion, garlic, ginger and chilli. Stir-fry over medium heat for 2–3 minutes. Add the curry powder and beef and stir-fry over high heat for 4–5 minutes, or until the beef is browned, then remove from the heat. Transfer the beef mixture to a bowl and add the potato and chopped coriander. Stir well, then season and set aside.

2 Lay the pastry sheets on a dry surface and cut out eight rounds, using a 7.5cm/3in pastry (cookie) cutter. Place a large spoonful of the beef mixture in the centre of each pastry round. Brush the edges with the beaten egg and fold each round in half. Press and crimp the edges with the tines of a fork to seal the edges together.

3 Fill a wok one-third full of oil and heat to 180°C/350°F (or until a cube of bread, dropped into the oil, browns in 15 seconds). Deep-fry the puffs, in batches, for 2–3 minutes until golden brown. Drain on kitchen paper, garnish with fresh coriander leaves and serve with tomato ketchup.

Nutritional information per portion: Energy 408kcal/1695kJ; Protein 9g; Carbohydrate 24.2g, of which sugars 1.8g; Fat 31.8g, of which saturates 4.2g; Cholesterol 67mg; Calcium 46mg; Fibre 0.5g; Sodium 202mg.

Fish and shellfish

Although chillies have a reputation for robust flavour, they can also be surprisingly subtle and combine well with many fish and shellfish dishes. In this chapter you'll find a marvellous range of mildly spiced and red hot dishes, from whole baked fish in simple sauces and creamy curries to fragrant noodles and aromatic risottos.

Tuna with chilli salad

Tuna steaks are wonderful seared and served with a punchy spicy sauce or salad. In this recipe the salad is flavoured with ginger, garlic and chillies, which perfectly complement the tuna.

SERVES 4

30ml/2 tbsp olive oil
5ml/1 tsp harissa
5ml/1 tsp clear honey
4 X 200g/7oz tuna steaks
salt and ground black pepper
lemon wedges, to serve

FOR THE SALAD
30ml/2 tbsp olive oil
a little butter
25g/1oz fresh root ginger, peeled and finely sliced
2 garlic cloves, finely sliced
2 green chillies, seeded and sliced
6 spring onions (scallions), cut into bitesize pieces
2 large handfuls of watercress
juice of 1/2 lemon

1 Mix the olive oil, harissa, honey and salt, and rub it over the tuna.

2 Heat a little oil in a frying pan and sear the tuna steaks for 2 minutes on each side.

3 Keep the tuna warm while you prepare the salad: heat the olive oil and butter in a pan. Add the ginger, garlic, chillies and spring onions, cook for a few minutes, then add the watercress.

4 When the watercress begins to darken and wilt, toss in the lemon juice and season well with salt and black pepper.

5 Transfer the warm salad on to a serving dish or individual plates. Slice the tuna steaks and arrange on top of the salad.

6 Serve the tuna salad immediately with chunky lemon wedges for squeezing over.

Nutritional information per portion: Energy 383kcal/1604kJ; Protein 48.1g; Carbohydrate 2g, of which sugars 2g; Fat 20.4g, of which saturates 4g; Cholesterol 56mg; Calcium 59mg; Fibre 0.4g; Sodium 102mg.

Chilli cod steaks

Cod has a delicate flavour and is the perfect fish to serve with a spicy sauce. These sizzling cod steaks would go well with some little boiled potatoes and green beans.

SERVES 4

4 cod or hake steaks
2 or 3 sprigs of fresh flat leaf parsley
4 slices white bread, toasted, then
crumbed in a food processor
salt and ground black pepper

FOR THE SAUCE
75–90ml/5–6 tbsp extra virgin olive oil
175ml/6fl oz/³⁄₄ cup white wine
2 garlic cloves, crushed
60ml/4 tbsp finely chopped flat
leaf parsley
1 fresh red or green chilli, seeded and
finely chopped
400g/14oz ripe tomatoes, peeled
and finely diced
salt and ground black pepper

1 Mix all the sauce ingredients in a bowl, and add some salt and pepper. Set the mixture aside.

2 Preheat the oven to 190°C/375°F/ Gas 5. Rinse the fish steaks then pat them dry with kitchen paper. Arrange them in a single layer in an oiled baking dish and sprinkle over the parsley. Season with salt and pepper. Then spoon the sauce evenly over each fish steak.

3 Sprinkle on half the breadcrumbs covering each steak well. Bake for 10 minutes, then baste with the juices in the dish.

4 Sprinkle the remaining breadcrumbs over the top of the dish. Return to the oven and bake for a further 10–15 minutes, until the fish are cooked and the breadcrumbs are crisp and have turned golden brown.

Nutritional information per portion: Energy 362kcal/1,510kJ; Protein 31g; Carbohydrate 13.1g, of which sugars 3.7g; Fat 17.9g, of which saturates 2.7g; Cholesterol 36mg; Calcium 49mg; Fibre 1.3g; Sodium 274mg.

Barbecued salmon with chilli

In this spicy Indian dish, the fish is cooked in a banana leaf parcel. The salmon really works well with the spices. Serve with freshly cooked rice or a green salad for a delicious main course.

SERVES 6

50g/2oz fresh coconut, skinned and finely grated, or 65g/2¹/₂oz/scant 1 cup desiccated (dry unsweetened shredded) coconut, soaked in 30ml/2 tbsp water

1 large lemon, skin, pith and seeds removed, chopped

4 large garlic cloves, crushed

3 large fresh mild green chillies, seeded and chopped

50g/2oz fresh coriander (cilantro), roughly chopped

25g/1oz fresh mint leaves, roughly chopped

5ml/1 tsp ground cumin

5ml/1 tsp sugar

2.5ml/¹/₂ tsp fenugreek seeds, finely ground

5ml/1 tsp salt

2 large, whole banana leaves

6 salmon fillets, total weight about 1.2kg/2¹/₂lb, skinned

1 Place all the ingredients except the banana leaves and salmon in a food processor or blender. Process or blend to a fine paste. Scrape the mixture into a bowl, cover and chill for 30 minutes.

2 To make the parcels, cut each banana leaf widthways into three and cut off the hard outer edges. Put the pieces of leaf and the edge strips in a bowl of hot water. Soak for 10 minutes. Drain, rinse, and pour over boiling water to soften. Drain, then place the leaves, smooth side up, on a board.

3 Smear the top and bottom of each with the coconut paste. Place one fillet on each banana leaf. Bring the trimmed edge of the leaf over the salmon, then fold in the sides. Bring up the remaining edge to make a neat parcel. Tie each parcel securely with a leaf strip.

4 Lay each parcel on a sheet of foil, bring up the edges and scrunch together to seal. Position a lightly oiled grill rack over a moderately hot barbecue. Place the salmon parcels on the grill rack and cook for about 10 minutes, turning over once.

5 Place on individual plates and leave to stand for 2–3 minutes. Remove the foil, then unwrap and eat the fish out of the parcel.

Nutritional information per portion: Energy 567kcal/2349kJ; Protein 34.9g; Carbohydrate 1g, of which sugars 0.8g; Fat 47.1g, of which saturates 7.5g; Cholesterol 113mg; Calcium 64mg; Fibre 0.6g; Sodium 1723mg.

Mackerel with red and green chillies

Oily fish such as mackerel is a perfect match for the clean, dry taste of sake. Garlic and chilli mute the strong flavour of the fish, while the mooli absorbs the flavours of the cooking liquid.

SERVES 2–3

1 large mackerel, filleted
300g/11oz mooli (daikon), peeled
120ml/4fl oz/½ cup light soy sauce
30ml/2 tbsp sake or rice wine
30ml/2 tbsp maple syrup
3 garlic cloves, crushed
10ml/2 tsp chilli powder
½ onion, chopped
1 fresh red chilli, seeded and
    finely sliced
1 fresh green chilli, seeded
    and finley sliced

1 Slice the mackerel into medium pieces. Cut the mooli into 2.5cm/1in cubes, and then arrange evenly across the base of a large pan. Cover with a layer of mackerel. Pour the soy sauce over the fish and add 200ml/7fl oz/ scant 1 cup water, the sake or rice wine, and the maple syrup.

2 Sprinkle the crushed garlic and chilli powder into the pan, and gently stir the liquid, trying not to disturb the fish and mooli. Add the chopped onion and sliced fresh red and green chillies, and cover the pan.

3 Place the pan over high heat and bring the liquid to the boil. Reduce the heat and simmer for 8–10 minutes, or until the fish is tender, spooning the soy liquid over the fish as it cooks.

4 Ladle the fish mixture into two or three individual oven-warmed serving bowls and serve immediately while hot.

Nutritional information per portion: Energy 207kcal/861kJ; Protein 13.4g; Carbohydrate 11.4g, of which sugars 10.9g; Fat 11g, of which saturates 2.3g; Cholesterol 36mg; Calcium 33mg; Fibre 1.2g; Sodium 81mg.

Sardines in spicy coconut milk

A deliciously spiced fish dish with a creamy coconut milk sauce. This dish is extremely fiery but its heat is tempered by the inclusion of fresh parsley and basil leaves.

SERVES 4

6–8 red chillies, according to taste, seeded and chopped
4 shallots, chopped
4 garlic cloves, chopped
1 lemon grass stalk, chopped
25g/1oz galangal, chopped
30ml/2 tbsp coconut or palm oil
10ml/2 tsp coriander seeds
5ml/1 tsp cumin seeds
5ml/1 tsp fennel seeds
1 bunch fresh mint leaves, chopped
1 bunch fresh flat leaf parsley, chopped
15ml/1 tbsp palm sugar (jaggery)
15ml/1 tbsp tamarind paste
4 sardines or small mackerel, gutted, but kept whole
300ml/1/2 pint/11/4 cups coconut milk
salt and ground black pepper
steamed rice, 1 large bunch fresh flat leaf parsley and fresh basil leaves, to serve

1 Using a mortar and pestle, pound the chillies, shallots, garlic, lemon grass and galangal to a paste. Heat the oil in a wok or pan, stir in the coriander, cumin and fennel seeds and fry until they give off a fragrant aroma.

2 Add the spicy paste and stir until it becomes golden in colour. Add the chopped mint and parsley and stir for about 1 minute, then add the sugar and tamarind paste.

3 Place the fish in the pan and toss gently to coat it in the paste. Pour in the coconut milk and stir gently. Bring to the boil, then reduce the heat and simmer the mixture for 10–15 minutes, until the fish is tender when flaked using a fork. Season the sauce with salt and ground black pepper to taste.

4 Cover the bottom of a warmed serving dish with sprigs of flat leaf parsley and place the fish on top, then spoon the sauce over the top. Serve with a bowl of steamed rice or sago and extra stalks of fresh parsley and basil leaves to cut the heat of the spice.

Nutritional information per portion: Energy 287kcal/1199kJ; Protein 22.8g; Carbohydrate 11g, of which sugars 10.2g; Fat 17.2g, of which saturates 3.7g; Cholesterol 0mg; Calcium 167mg; Fibre 2.1g; Sodium 213mg.

Sardines stuffed with chilli

Chillies are the perfect ingredient for making a paste. In this very simple, traditional Italian recipe, fresh sardines or plump, overgrown anchovies are stuffed with a succulent, spicy filling.

SERVES 4

2–3 stale crusty white bread rolls,
   crusts removed
about 120ml/4fl oz/¹/₂ cup milk
40 fresh sardines or large anchovies,
   scaled and filleted
3 eggs, beaten
45ml/3 tbsp freshly grated
   Parmesan cheese
2 garlic cloves, chopped
a handful of fresh flat leaf parsley,
   leaves chopped
1 dried red chilli
about 90ml/6 tbsp plain
   (all-purpose) flour
about 2 litres/3¹/₂ pints/9 cups
   sunflower oil, for deep-frying
sea salt

1 Soak the bread in the milk to cover, then squeeze dry. Use any damaged fish fillets for the filling. Put all the perfectly shaped fillets to one side.

2 Mix the bread with the damaged fish, half the beaten eggs, the grated Parmesan cheese, garlic, parsley, chilli and a pinch of salt. Blend it all together to make a firm paste with your hands or a fork.

3 Sandwich two fillets together with a generous spoonful of the filling in the middle, then gently coat in the remaining beaten egg and then the flour. Repeat this process for the remaining fillets.

4 Heat the oil in large pan until sizzling, then fry the fish, in batches, until crisp and golden brown; about 2 minutes. Drain on kitchen paper and serve hot.

Nutritional information per portion: Energy 621kcal/2594kJ; Protein 35.8g; Carbohydrate 37.2g, of which sugars 2.6g; Fat 37.7g, of which saturates 9.3g; Cholesterol 155mg; Calcium 343mg; Fibre 1.3g; Sodium 505mg.

Chilli marinated steamed sea bass

*Vinegar, chilli and garlic add spice and piquancy to this colourful fish dish that tastes every
bit as good as it looks. The fish is steamed in a pan, and is ideal for entertaining.*

SERVES 2

**1 sea bass, weighing about 500g/1¹/₄lb,
scaled and cleaned**

2.5ml/¹/₂ tsp ground black pepper

2.5ml/¹/₂ tsp ground cumin

45ml/3 tbsp red wine vinegar

75ml/5 tbsp vegetable oil

1 large red onion, chopped

1 small tomato, chopped

1 small piece of red (bell) pepper, diced

1 chilli, seeded and finely chopped

15ml/1 tbsp grated garlic

10ml/2 tsp paprika

salt

boiled cassava, to serve

1 Season the sea bass with pepper,
cumin and salt. Add the vinegar and
leave to marinate for 15 minutes.

2 Heat the oil in a frying pan and fry
the onion for 5 minutes. When it
starts to brown, add the chopped
tomato, diced pepper, chopped
chilli, garlic and paprika and cook for
a further 5 minutes.

3 Lay the fish in the pan and pour in
its seasonings and vinegar. Cover the
pan and leave the fish to steam for
15 minutes at medium heat.

4 Using a fork, carefully check that
the fish is cooked: if the flesh flakes
easily, remove from the heat. Serve
the fish accompanied by boiled
cassava, if using.

Nutritional information per portion: Energy 592kcal/2471kJ; Protein 50.6g; Carbohydrate 27.8g, of which sugars 21.2g;
Fat 31.8g, of which saturates 4g; Cholesterol 120mg; Calcium 77mg; Fibre 5.7g; Sodium 750mg.

Chilli-flavoured sea bass

This tasty dish, known as ceviche, is particularly popular in Peru, where it is made with a variety of fish and shellfish. The raw fish simply 'cooks' in a chilli-flavoured fresh citrus marinade, and needs no heating, so it is vital that the fish is perfectly fresh.

SERVES 4

675g/1¹/₂lb sea bass fillets
300ml/¹/₂ pint/1¹/₄ cups lime juice
200ml/7 fl oz/scant 1 cup orange juice
2 fresh red chillies, seeded and
   finely sliced
1 medium red onion, finely sliced
30ml/2 tbsp fresh coriander
   (cilantro) leaves
1 large tomato, seeded and chopped
salt and ground black pepper
green salad and crusty bread,
   to serve

1 Cut the sea bass fillets into 2.5cm/ 1in strips, removing any bones with tweezers. Place the fish in a bowl and season with salt and pepper.

2 Pour the lime juice and orange juice over the fish, then gently stir in the sliced chillies and onion slices. The fish must be totally immersed in the marinade.

3 Cover the bowl with clear film (plastic wrap) and place it in the refrigerator to chill for at least 2 hours, until the fish becomes opaque in colour.

4 Stir the coriander leaves and the chopped tomato into the fish mixture. Serve with a green salad and crusty bread.

Nutritional information per portion: Energy 216kcal/908kJ; Protein 33.9g; Carbohydrate 10.3g, of which sugars 9.1g; Fat 4.6g, of which saturates 0.8g; Cholesterol 135mg; Calcium 241mg; Fibre 1.4g; Sodium 129mg.

Grilled hake with lemon and chilli

Sometimes it is the simplest dishes that make the most impact. This dish not only looks pretty, but tastes delicious, with crushed chilli flakes giving it character. Choose firm hake fillets, as thick as possible, and serve with new potatoes or creamy mash and steamed fine green beans.

SERVES 4

4 hake fillets, each 150g/5oz
30ml/2 tbsp olive oil
finely grated rind and juice
    of 1 unwaxed lemon
15ml/1 tbsp crushed chilli flakes
salt and ground black pepper

1 Preheat the grill (broiler) to high. Brush the hake fillets all over with the olive oil and place them skin side up on a baking sheet.

2 Grill (broil) the hake fillets for 4–5 minutes, until the skin is crispy, then carefully turn them over.

3 Sprinkle the fillets with the lemon rind and chilli flakes and season with salt and ground black pepper.

4 Grill the fillets for a further 2–3 minutes, or until the hake is cooked through. Squeeze over the lemon juice just before serving.

Nutritional information per portion: Energy 188kcal/786kJ; Protein 27g; Carbohydrate 0.1g, of which sugars 0.1g; Fat 8.8g, of which saturates 1.2g; Cholesterol 35mg; Calcium 22mg; Fibre 0g; Sodium 150mg.

Roasted fish with chillies and walnuts

This spicy dish is a favourite along the coast of Lebanon. Traditionally dogfish is used, but any firm-fleshed fish, such as trout, sea bass or snapper, is ideal. Topped with a chilli tahini sauce, this dish is spectacular when garnished with refreshing pomegranate seeds.

SERVES 4

2 x 900g/2lb firm-fleshed fish, gutted
    and cleaned
60ml/4 tbsp olive oil
2 onions, finely chopped
1 green (bell) pepper, finely chopped
1–2 red chillies, seeded and very
    finely chopped
115g/4oz walnuts, finely chopped
15–30ml/1–2 tbsp pomegranate molasses
small bunch of fresh coriander (cilantro),
    finely chopped
small bunch of flat leaf parsley,
    finely chopped
sea salt and ground black pepper
seeds of ¹/₂ pomegranate, with pith
    removed, to garnish

FOR THE SAUCE

60ml/4 tbsp tahini
juice of 1 lemon
juice of 1 orange
15ml/1 tbsp olive oil
2 cloves garlic, finely chopped
1–2 red chillies, seeded and chopped
sea salt and ground black pepper

1 Using a sharp knife, make three or four diagonal slits on each side of the fish. Rub the cavity with salt and pepper, cover the fish and chill for 30 minutes.

2 Meanwhile, prepare the filling. Heat 30ml/2 tbsp olive oil in a heavy pan and fry the onions, pepper, and chillies until lightly browned.

3 Stir in the walnuts and pomegranate molasses and add half the coriander and parsley. Season to taste and leave the filling to cool. Preheat the oven to 200°C/400°F/Gas 6.

4 Fill the fish with the stuffing and secure the opening with a wooden skewer or cocktail sticks (toothpicks). Place the fish in an oiled baking dish and pour over the remaining oil. Bake in the preheated oven for about 30 minutes.

5 Meanwhile, to make the sauce, beat the tahini with the lemon and orange juice in a small bowl or jug (pitcher), adding a little water if necessary, until the mixture is smooth and creamy.

6 Heat the olive oil in a small frying pan and stir in the garlic and chillies, until they begin to colour. Stir in the tahini mixture and heat it through. Season with salt and pepper and keep warm.

7 Transfer the cooked fish to a serving dish and drizzle some of the sauce over the top. Garnish with the pomegranate seeds and serve immediately with the rest of the sauce served separately.

Nutritional information per portion: Energy 772kcal/3223kJ; Protein 78.8g; Carbohydrate 13.1g, of which sugars 10.3g; Fat 45.3g, of which saturates 6.5g; Cholesterol 288mg; Calcium 292mg; Fibre 4.9g; Sodium 276mg

Fried fish with chilli

Garlic, chilli and tomatoes make a winning combination, adding colour and a spicy topping to fried fish. This appetizing dish tastes every bit as good as it looks.

SERVES 6

**6 white fish fillets, such as cod, haddock
  or sea bass**
50g/2oz plain (all-purpose) flour
250ml/8fl oz/1 cup vegetable oil
3 medium red onions, sliced into rings
3 garlic cloves, finely chopped
**4 medium tomatoes, peeled, seeded
  and diced**
**2 fresh chillies, seeded and thinly
  cut lengthways**
15ml/1 tbsp chilli sauce
2.5ml/½ tsp dried oregano
juice of 1 lime
salt and ground black pepper
parsley leaves, to garnish
rice or boiled potatoes, to serve

1 Season the fish with salt and pepper and dust with flour. Heat the oil in a frying pan, reserving 30ml/2 tbsp, and fry the fillets, turning once, until golden and cooked through. Transfer them to a plate and keep warm.

2 Heat the remaining oil over medium heat and fry the onions until they are browned.

3 Add the garlic, tomatoes, chilli strips and chilli sauce and the oregano. Cook for 5 minutes.

4 Spoon the onion and tomato mixture into a serving dish and lay the fish on top, or transfer the sauce to a bowl and serve on the side. Sprinkle the fish with lime juice and garnish with parsley. Serve with rice or boiled potatoes.

Nutritional information per portion: Energy 412kcal/1712kJ; Protein 29.6g; Carbohydrate 14.6g, of which sugars 6.3g; Fat 26.5g, of which saturates 2.8g; Cholesterol 69mg; Calcium 50mg; Fibre 1.9g; Sodium 97mg.

Spicy fish stew

Satisfying, spicy and simple to prepare, this recipe, from northern Peru, uses coriander, garlic and ginger to flavour the hot chilli sauce which is used to marinate the fish.

SERVES 6

6 white fish fillets, such as cod
1 large red onion, sliced lengthways
1 red (bell) pepper, thinly sliced
3 garlic cloves
2.5cm/1in piece fresh root ginger
100g/3³⁄₄oz fresh coriander (cilantro)
1.5ml/¹⁄₄ tsp ground cumin
45ml/3 tbsp chilli sauce
120ml/4fl oz/¹⁄₂ cup vegetable oil
120ml/4fl oz/¹⁄₂ cup white beer
250g/9oz/2 cups shelled peas
juice of 1 lime
salt and ground black pepper
boiled rice, to serve

1 Arrange the fish fillets in a wide pan and cover with the slices of onion and red pepper.

2 Put the garlic, ginger, coriander, cumin, chilli sauce and oil into a blender or food processor and blend to a purée. Spoon over the fish and leave to marinate for 15 minutes.

3 Put the pan on high heat until the fish sizzles, pour in the beer and add the peas and bring to the boil. Reduce the heat, cover the pan and simmer for 15 minutes.

4 When the fish is cooked, squeeze the lime juice over the top, and serve with rice.

Nutritional information per portion: Energy 302kcal/1257kJ; Protein 31.5g; Carbohydrate 9.6g, of which sugars 5.4g; Fat 14.9g, of which saturates 1.6g; Cholesterol 69mg; Calcium 63mg; Fibre 3.5g; Sodium 183mg.

Chilli escabeche

In this red-hot version of the Mediterranean classic, fish is fried and covered with a thick, spicy and tangy sauce, which gets its sizzle from the combination of red chillies, chilli sauce and cumin.

SERVES 4

2 medium onions
500ml/17fl oz/generous 2 cups water
175ml/6fl oz/^{3}/$_4$ cup red wine vinegar
500g/1^1/$_4$lb firm-textured fish
   fillets, such as sea bass, bream,
   cod or haddock
115g/4oz plain (all-purpose) flour
200ml/7fl oz/scant 1 cup vegetable oil
4 garlic cloves
2 red chillies, seeded and sliced
   lengthways

30ml/2 tbsp red chilli sauce
2.5ml/^{1}/$_2$ tsp ground cumin
2 medium sweet potatoes
4 lettuce leaves
8–10 olives
115g/4oz feta cheese.
2 hard-boiled eggs, sliced
salt and ground black pepper

1 Thickly slice the onions lengthways and put them in a large pan with the water, and 50ml/2fl oz/ ^{1}/$_4$ cup of the red wine vinegar. Add a good pinch of salt. Bring the pan to the boil and then reduce to a simmer for 2 minutes. Remove the pan from the heat, drain the onions and set aside.

2 Cut the fish fillets into four portions. Season the flour with pepper and salt and toss the fish in it until it is coated well in the flour.

3 Heat 150ml/^{1}/$_4$ pint/^{2}/$_3$ cup of the vegetable oil in a frying pan over medium heat and fry the fish for about 6 minutes on each side, until cooked through, then lift the pieces out and arrange them in a shallow dish.

4 Finely chop the garlic. Slice the chillies in half, carefully scrape out all the seeds and slice lengthways into fine strips.

5 Add the remaining oil to the frying pan over medium-high heat. Add the chopped garlic, and fry until golden. Add the boiled onions, the sliced chillies, chilli sauce and cumin, stir and add the rest of the red wine vinegar.

6 Check the seasoning, adding more salt if necessary. Remove the frying pan from the heat and pour the sauce all over the fish fillets. Put to one side and leave to cool.

7 Put the sweet potatoes in a large pan with enough water to cover and boil them for 25 minutes, until they are tender. Once they are cooked, drain the potatoes and peel and slice them.

8 Place a lettuce leaf on each serving plate and spoon a portion of fish with some of the sauce on top. Add slices of sweet potato and garnish each plate with a couple of olives. Crumble some feta on top and add a couple of slices of hard-boiled egg. Serve.

Nutritional information per portion: Energy 414kcal/1720kJ; Protein 41.9g; Carbohydrate 1.3g, of which sugars 1g; Fat 26.7g, of which saturates 3.2g; Cholesterol 104mg; Calcium 30mg; Fibre 0.2g; Sodium 137mg.

Green fish curry

Any firm-fleshed fish can be used in this spicy dish, which gains its rich flavour from a mixture of fresh herbs, spices, lime and fresh chillies. A garnish of green chilli slices gives it extra heat.

SERVES 4

4 garlic cloves, coarsely chopped

5cm/2in piece fresh root ginger, peeled
 and coarsely chopped

2 fresh green chillies, seeded and
 coarsely chopped

grated rind and juice of 1 lime

5–10ml/1–2 tsp shrimp paste (optional)

5ml/1 tsp coriander seeds

5ml/1 tsp five-spice powder

75ml/6 tbsp sesame oil

2 red onions, finely chopped

900g/2lb hoki fillets, skinned

400ml/14fl oz/1²/₃ cups canned
 coconut milk

45ml/3 tbsp Thai fish sauce

50g/2oz/2 cups fresh coriander
 (cilantro) leaves

50g/2oz/2 cups fresh basil leaves

6 spring onions (scallions),
 coarsely chopped

150ml/¹/₄ pint/²/₃ cup sunflower or
 groundnut (peanut) oil

sliced fresh green chilli and finely
 chopped fresh coriander (cilantro),
 to garnish

cooked basmati or Thai fragrant rice
 and lime wedges, to serve

1 First make the curry paste. Combine the garlic, ginger, chillies, lime juice and shrimp paste, if using, in a food processor. Add the spices, with half the sesame oil. Process to a paste, then spoon into a bowl, cover and set aside.

2 Heat a wok or large, shallow pan, and pour in the remaining sesame oil. When it is hot, stir-fry the red onions over high heat for 2 minutes. Add the fish and stir-fry for 1–2 minutes to seal the fillets on all sides.

3 Lift out the red onions and fish with a slotted spoon and put them on a plate. Add the curry paste to the wok or pan and fry for 1 minute, stirring constantly. Return the fish and onions to the pan, pour in the coconut milk and bring to the boil. Lower the heat, add the Thai fish sauce and simmer gently for 5–7 minutes until the fish is cooked through and tender.

4 Process the herbs, spring onions, lime rind and sunflower or groundnut oil to a coarse paste. Stir into the fish curry. Garnish with chilli and coriander and serve with rice and lime wedges.

Nutritional information per portion: Energy 575kcal/2390kJ; Protein 40g; Carbohydrate 6.2g, of which sugars 4.9g; Fat 43.5g, of which saturates 5.9g; Cholesterol 6mg; Calcium 132mg; Fibre 0g; Sodium 362mg.

Eel in a chilli caramel sauce

The flesh of an eel is very rich and firm and has a wonderful flavour which combines well with chillies. The fat rendered from the eel melts into the spicy sauce, making it deliciously velvety.

SERVES 4

45ml/3 tbsp raw cane sugar
30ml/2 tbsp soy sauce
45ml/3 tbsp nuoc mam
2 garlic cloves, crushed
2 dried chillies
2–3 star anise
4–5 black peppercorns
350g/12oz eel on the bone, skinned, cut
    into 2.5cm/1in chunks
200g/7oz butternut squash, cut into
    bitesize chunks
4 spring onions (scallions), cut into
    bitesize pieces
30ml/2 tbsp sesame oil
5cm/2in fresh root ginger, peeled
    and cut into matchsticks
salt
cooked rice, to serve

1 Put the raw cane sugar in a wok or heavy pan with 30ml/2 tbsp water, and gently heat until the sugar melts and the thick syrup turns a golden colour.

2 Remove the wok or pan from the heat. Add the soy sauce and the nuoc mam with 120ml/4fl oz/1/2 cup water to make the sauce and mix well.

3 Add the crushed garlic, dried chillies, star anise and black peppercorns to the sauce. Return the pan to the heat. Add the eel chunks, butternut squash and spring onions, coating the eel in the sauce, and season with salt.

4 Reduce the heat, cover the pan and simmer gently for about 20 minutes, until the eel and vegetables are tender.

5 Meanwhile, heat a small wok, pour in the oil and stir-fry the ginger until crisp and golden. Remove and drain on kitchen paper. Serve the eel with rice, with the crispy ginger sprinkled on top.

Nutritional information per portion: Energy 204Kcal/857kJ; Protein 11g; Carbohydrate 20g, of which sugars 14g; Fat 10g, of which saturates 1g; Cholesterol 0mg; Calcium 76mg; Fibre 1g; Sodium 110mg.

Fiery prawn noodles

*In Malaysia and Singapore, there are endless stir-fried noodle dishes. The rice vermicelli in
this sizzling snack are stir-fried with prawns and a plenty of fresh and dried chillies.*

SERVES 4

30ml/2 tbsp vegetable oil
1 carrot, cut into matchsticks
225g/8oz fresh prawns (shrimp), peeled
120ml/4fl oz/¹/₂ cup chicken stock
30ml/2 tbsp light soy sauce
15ml/1 tbsp dark soy sauce
175g/6oz beansprouts
115g/4oz mustard greens or pak choi
   (bok choy), shredded
225g/8oz dried rice vermicelli, soaked in
   warm water until pliable, and drained
1–2 fresh red chillies, seeded and finely
   sliced, and fresh coriander (cilantro)
   leaves, roughly chopped, to garnish

FOR THE SPICE PASTE

4 dried red chillies
25g/1oz fresh root ginger
4 garlic cloves, chopped
4 shallots, chopped
5ml/1 tsp ground turmeric

1 First make the spice paste. Soak the dried red chillies in water until soft,
then slice them in half and carefully remove the seeds using a knife and fork.
Peel and chop the ginger into small pieces.

2 Place all the ingredients for the spice paste in a mortar and pestle or food
processor or blender and grind or process to a smooth paste.

3 Heat the vegetable oil in a wok or pan and stir in the spice paste. Add the
carrot matchsticks to the pan and cook, stirring constantly, for a minute.
Then add the prawns to the pan and mix well.

4 Pour in the stock and the soy sauces and mix well until it is combined.
Cook for about 1–2 minutes over medium heat. Add the beansprouts and
mustard greens or pak choi to the pan, followed by the vermicelli.

5 Toss well to make sure the vegetables and vermicelli are well coated and
heated through. Transfer to a warmed serving plate. Garnish with the sliced
chillies and coriander.

Nutritional information per portion: Energy 330kcal/1377kJ; Protein 17.5g; Carbohydrate 49.9g, of which sugars 4.5g;
Fat 6.6g, of which saturates 0.8g; Cholesterol 110mg; Calcium 125mg; Fibre 1.9g; Sodium 960mg.

Chilli prawns with creamy coconut

The prawns are cooked in a luxurious coconut milk sauce, which gives this dish a wonderful flavour. Serve this with cooked white rice and sprigs of fresh coriander.

SERVES 6

130g/4¹/₂oz/2¹/₄ cups white breadcrumbs
105ml/7 tbsp coconut milk
30 raw king prawns (jumbo shrimp), about
    900g/2lb, peeled, reserving the shells
400ml/14fl oz/1²/₃ cups fish stock
2 large tomatoes, roughly chopped
1 onion, quartered
2 fresh red chillies, seeded and
    roughly chopped
130g/4¹/₂oz dried shrimps
45ml/3 tbsp palm oil
2 garlic cloves, crushed
25g/1oz fresh root ginger, grated
75g/3oz/³/₄ cup roasted peanuts
50g/2oz/¹/₂ cup cashew nuts
60ml/4 tbsp coconut cream
juice of 1 lime
salt and ground black pepper
cooked rice and fresh coriander, to serve

1 Place the breadcrumbs in a bowl and stir in the coconut milk. Leave to soak for 30 minutes. Purée, in a blender or food processor, then scrape into a bowl and set aside.

2 Place the prawn shells in a pan and add the fish stock and tomatoes. Bring to the boil, then simmer for 30 minutes. Strain the stock into a bowl.

3 Put the onion, chillies and dried shrimps in a blender or food processor and purée. Scrape into a pan and stir in the palm oil.

4 Cook over low heat for 5 minutes. Add the garlic and ginger and cook for 2 minutes.

5 Grind the peanuts and cashew nuts in a food processor until they become a fine powder. Stir into the pan and cook for about 1 minute.

6 Stir in the coconut purée and prawn stock and bring to the boil. Reduce the heat and cook, stirring for 6–8 minutes. Add the coconut cream, lime juice and prawns. Cook for 3 minutes until the prawns are cooked. Season and serve.

Nutritional information per portion: Energy 204Kcal/857kJ; Protein 11g; Carbohydrate 20g, of which sugars 14g; Fat 10g, of which saturates 1g; Cholesterol 0mg; Calcium 76mg; Fibre 1g; Sodium 110mg.

Spicy shrimp and potato stew

New potatoes with plenty of flavour are essential for this effortless warming stew. Use a good quality jar of tomato and chilli sauce; there are now plenty available in the supermarkets.

SERVES 4

675g/1½lb small new potatoes

15g/½oz/½ cup fresh coriander (cilantro)

350g/12oz jar tomato and chilli sauce

300g/11oz cooked peeled prawns (shrimp), thawed and drained if frozen

1 Wash and scrub the new potatoes. Fill a large pan with a lid with lightly salted boiling water and cook the potatoes for 15 minutes, until tender. Drain and return the cooked potatoes to the pan.

2 Chop half the coriander and add to the pan. Add the tomato and chilli sauce to the pan with 90ml/ 6 tbsp water, and bring to the boil.

3 Cover the pan with the lid and reduce the heat and simmer gently for 5 minutes.

4 Stir in the prawns and heat briefly until they are warmed through. Do not overheat the prawns or they will quickly shrivel, becoming tough. Spoon into shallow bowls and serve sprinkled with the remaining coriander, torn into pieces.

Nutritional information per portion: Energy 218kcal/924kJ; Protein 16.9g; Carbohydrate 30.4g, of which sugars 5.4g; Fat 4.1g, of which saturates 0.7g; Cholesterol 146mg; Calcium 84mg; Fibre 2.9g; Sodium 171mg.

Spicy yellow prawn curry

This scorchingly hot curry is a real taste sensation. This creamy dish originates from Indonesia and is very easy to make. Big, juicy fresh prawns are used, but you can easily substitute them with scallops, squid or mussels, or a combination of all three, depending on what you have available.

SERVES 4

2 shallots
2 garlic cloves
25g/1oz fresh root ginger
2 red chillies
30ml/2 tbsp coconut or
    palm oil
2 lemon grass stalks, finely sliced
10ml/2 tsp ground turmeric
10ml/2 tsp coriander seeds
10ml/2 tsp shrimp paste
1 red (bell) pepper, seeded and
    finely sliced
4 kaffir lime leaves

about 500g/1¼lb fresh
    prawns (shrimp), shelled
    and deveined
400g/14oz can coconut milk
salt and ground black pepper
1 green chilli, seeded and sliced,
    to garnish
4 fried shallots or fresh chillies,
    seeded and sliced lengthways and
    cooked rice, to serve

1 Finely chop the shallots, garlic cloves and ginger. Slice the red chillies in half and carefully remove the seeds with a knife and fork, and finely chop.

2 Heat the oil in a wok or heavy frying pan. Add the shallots, garlic, ginger, chillies to the pan and stir well. Finely slice the lemon grass and add to the pan with the ground turmeric and coriander seeds. Fry until fragrant.

3 Stir in the shrimp paste and cook the mixture for 2–3 minutes. Add the red pepper and lime leaves and stir-fry for a further 1 minute.

4 Add the prawns to the pan. Pour in the coconut milk, stirring to combine, and bring to the boil. Cook for 5–6 minutes until the prawns are cooked. Season with salt and pepper to taste.

5 Spoon the cooked prawns on to a warmed serving dish and sprinkle with the sliced green chillies to garnish. Serve with rice and fried shallots or the fresh chillies on the side.

Nutritional information per portion: Energy 230kcal/965kJ; Protein 26.4g; Carbohydrate 16g, of which sugars 13.5g; Fat 7.2g, of which saturates 1g; Cholesterol 263mg; Calcium 226mg; Fibre 2.7g; Sodium 519mg.

Octopus in chilli sauce

Here octopus is stir-fried to give it a rich meaty texture, then smothered in a fiery chilli sauce. The dish combines the charred octopus flavour with the zing of jalapeño chillies.

SERVES 2

2 small octopuses, cleaned and gutted
15ml/1 tbsp vegetable oil
1/2 onion, sliced 5mm/1/4in thick
1/4 carrot, thinly sliced
1/2 leek, thinly sliced
75g/3oz jalapeño chillies, trimmed
2 garlic cloves, crushed
10ml/2 tsp chilli powder
5ml/1 tsp dark soy sauce
45ml/3 tbsp chilli paste
30ml/2 tbsp mirin or rice wine
15ml/1 tbsp maple syrup
sesame oil and sesame seeds,
    to garnish
cooked white rice, to serve

1 Fill a large pan with water and bring to the boil. Blanch the octopuses in the boiling water to soften slightly. Drain well, and cut the octopuses into pieces approximately 5cm/2in long.

2 Heat the oil in a large frying pan over medium-high heat and add the onion, carrot, leek and jalapeño chillies. Stir-fry for 3 minutes.

3 Add the octopus, garlic, and the chilli powder. Stir-fry for 3–4 minutes, or until the octopus is tender. Add the soy sauce, chilli paste, mirin or rice wine, and maple syrup. Mix well and stir-fry for 1 minute more.

4 Transfer to a serving platter, drizzle with sesame oil and a sprinkling of sesame seeds. Serve with rice.

Nutritional information per portion: Energy 235kcal/988kJ; Protein 28.6g; Carbohydrate 13.2g, of which sugars 11.9g; Fat 8g, of which saturates 1.2g; Cholesterol 72mg; Calcium 76mg; Fibre 2.4g; Sodium 204mg.

Spicy sweet and sour squid

This is a delicious way to cook squid. The sweet soy sauce and the kick of the chillies is divine with these scrumptious baby squid, and the aroma during cooking will make your mouth water.

SERVES 3–4

500g/1½lb fresh baby squid
30ml/2 tbsp tamarind paste
30ml/2 tbsp chilli sauce
45ml/3 tbsp sweet soy sauce
juice of 1 lime
25g/1oz fresh root ginger, grated
1 small bunch fresh coriander
   (cilantro) leaves
2–4 green chillies, seeded and
   quartered lengthways
ground black pepper
fresh coriander (cilantro) leaves,
   to serve

1 Clean the squid and remove the head and ink sac. Pull out the backbone and rinse the body sac inside and out. Trim the head above the eyes, keeping the tentacle intact. Carefully dry the body sac and tentacles on kitchen paper and discard the rest.

2 In a bowl, mix together the tamarind paste, chilli sauce, sweet soy sauce and lime juice. Add the ginger and a little black pepper.

3 Spoon the sauce mixture over the squid and rub it all over the body sacs and tentacles so it is covered well in the sauce. Cover and chill for 1 hour.

4 Meanwhile, prepare the barbecue or heat a ridged griddle. Place the squid on the rack or griddle and cook for 3 minutes on each side, brushing them with the marinade as they cook. Serve immediately, with fresh coriander leaves.

Nutritional information per portion: Energy 110kcal/468kJ; Protein 20g; Carbohydrate 2.8g, of which sugars 1.1g; Fat 2.3g, of which saturates 0.5g; Cholesterol 281mg; Calcium 43mg; Fibre 0.6g; Sodium 943mg.

Spicy squid casserole

This fiery stew is the ideal dish to have on a cold evening. The potatoes disintegrate to thicken and enrich the intense chilli sauce, making a blistering-hot and substantial main course. For a heartier dish with a richer flavour, use cabernet sauvignon in place of the white wine.

SERVES 6

800g/1³/₄lb squid
45ml/3 tbsp olive oil
5 garlic cloves, crushed
4 fresh jalapeño chillies, seeded and
   finely chopped
2 celery sticks, diced
500g/1¹/₄lb small new potatoes or baby
   salad potatoes, scrubbed, scraped or
   peeled and quartered

400ml/14fl oz/1²/₃ cups dry
   white wine
400ml/14fl oz/1²/₃ cups
   fish stock
4 tomatoes, diced
30ml/2 tbsp chopped fresh flat
   leaf parsley
salt
white rice or corn breads, to serve

1 Clean the squid under cold water. Pull the tentacles away from the body. The squid's entrails will come out easily. Remove the cartilage from inside the body cavity and discard it. Wash the body thoroughly.

2 Pull away the membrane that covers the body. Cut between the tentacles and head, discarding the head and entrails. Leave the tentacles whole but discard the hard beak in the middle. Cut the body into thin rounds.

3 Heat the oil, add the garlic, chillies and celery and cook for 5 minutes. Stir in the potatoes, then add the wine and stock. Bring to the boil, then simmer, covered, for 25 minutes.

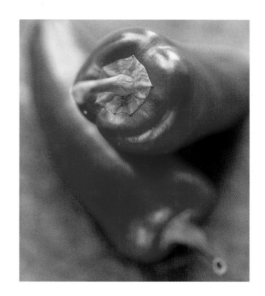

4 Remove the pan from the heat and stir in the squid, tomatoes and parsley. Cover the pan and leave to stand until the squid is cooked. Serve immediately with rice or corn breads if using.

Nutritional information per portion: Energy 281kcal/1183kJ; Protein 23.3g; Carbohydrate 18.7g, of which sugars 4.8g; Fat 8.4g, of which saturates 1.5g; Cholesterol 300mg; Calcium 44mg; Fibre 2g; Sodium 175mg.

Squid risotto with chilli and coriander

Squid needs to be cooked either very quickly or very slowly. Here the squid is seasoned overnight in a fruity and spicy marinade – a popular method in New Zealand for tenderizing squid.

SERVES 3–4

450g/1lb squid body sac and tentacles
45ml/3 tbsp olive oil
15g/½oz/1 tbsp butter
1 onion, finely chopped
2 garlic cloves, crushed
1 fresh red chilli, seeded and finely sliced
275g/10oz/1½ cups risotto rice
175ml/6fl oz/¾ cup dry white wine
1 litre/1¾ pints/4 cups hot fish stock

30ml/2 tbsp chopped fresh
    coriander (cilantro)
salt and ground black pepper

FOR THE MARINADE
2 ripe kiwi fruit, chopped and mashed
1 fresh red chilli, seeded and finely sliced
30ml/2 tbsp fresh lime juice

1 Mix all the marinade ingredients in a bowl, then add the squid, stirring to coat. Season, cover with clear film (plastic wrap) and leave in the refrigerator for 4 hours or overnight.

2 Drain the squid. Heat 15ml/1 tbsp of the oil in a frying pan and cook the strips, in batches if necessary, for 30–60 seconds over high heat. It is important that the squid cooks very quickly. Transfer to a plate and set aside. Don't worry if some of the marinade clings to the squid, but if too much juice accumulates in the pan, pour this into a jug (pitcher) and add more olive oil when cooking the next batch so that the squid fries rather than simmers. Reserve the accumulated juices in the jug.

3 Heat the remaining oil with the butter in a large pan and gently fry the onion and garlic for 5–6 minutes until soft. Add the chilli and fry for 1 minute, then add the rice. Cook for a few minutes, stirring, until the rice is coated with oil and slightly translucent.

4 Stir in the wine until it is absorbed. Gradually add the stock and reserved cooking liquid from the squid, a ladleful at a time, stirring constantly and waiting until each quantity of stock has been absorbed before adding the next.

5 After 15 minutes, stir in the squid and continue cooking the risotto until all the stock has been absorbed and the rice is tender, but still firm to the bite. Stir in the chopped coriander, cover with the lid or a dish towel, and leave to rest for a few minutes before serving.

Nutritional information per portion: Energy 663kcal/2771kJ; Protein 31.9g; Carbohydrate 79g, of which sugars 7.3g; Fat 19.4g, of which saturates 4.8g; Cholesterol 348mg; Calcium 63mg; Fibre 1.5g; Sodium 204mg.

Mussel risotto with green chillies

Fresh root ginger and coriander add a distinctive flavour to this dish, while the fresh green chillies provide the heat. Use jalapeños or serranos for a seriously fiery dish.

SERVES 3–4

**900g/2lb fresh mussels, scrubbed
clean, discarding any that do not
close when sharply tapped**
**about 250ml/8fl oz/1 cup dry
white wine**
30ml/2 tbsp olive oil
1 onion, chopped
2 garlic cloves, crushed
**1–2 fresh green chillies, seeded
and finely sliced**
2.5cm/1in piece of fresh root ginger, grated
275g/10oz/1$\frac{1}{2}$ cups risotto rice
**900ml/1$\frac{1}{2}$ pints/3$\frac{3}{4}$ cups
simmering fish stock**
**30ml/2 tbsp chopped fresh
coriander (cilantro)**
30ml/2 tbsp double (heavy) cream
salt and ground black pepper

1 Place the mussels in a large pan. Add 120ml/4fl oz/$\frac{1}{2}$ cup of the wine and bring to the boil. Cover and cook for 4–5 minutes. Drain, reserving the liquid and discarding any mussels that have not opened. Remove most of the mussels from their shells, reserving a few in their shells for a garnish. Strain the mussel liquid.

2 Heat the oil in pan and fry the onion and garlic for 3–4 minutes until it softens. Add the chillies. Continue for 1–2 minutes, stir in the ginger and fry for 1 minute more. Add the risotto rice and cook over medium heat for 2 minutes. Stir in the reserved cooking liquid. Once absorbed, add the remaining wine and cook, stirring, until this has been absorbed. Add the fish stock, a little at a time.

3 After 15 minutes, stir in the mussels, then add the coriander and season. Add the stock to the risotto until it is creamy and the rice is tender. Remove from the heat, stir in the double cream. Spoon into a warmed serving dish, garnish with the reserved mussels in their shells, and serve immediately.

Nutritional information per portion: Energy 439kcal/1833kJ; Protein 17.2g; Carbohydrate 56.6g, of which sugars 1.4g; Fat 11.3g, of which saturates 3.5g; Cholesterol 37mg; Calcium 159mg; Fibre 0.2g; Sodium 146mg.

Spicy paella rice

This version of the Spanish classic has acquired some spicy touches. The trick is to use enough chilli to make it lively, but not so much that you can't taste the meat, fish and shellfish.

SERVES 6

150g/5oz prepared squid, cut into rings
275g/10oz cod or haddock fillets
8–10 raw king prawns (jumbo shrimp)
8 scallops, trimmed and halved
2 skinless chicken breast fillets
350g/12oz fresh mussels
250g/9oz/1⅓ cups long grain rice
30ml/2 tbsp sunflower oil
2 courgettes (zucchini)
1 red (bell) pepper
400ml/14fl oz/1⅔ cups chicken stock
250ml/8fl oz/1 cup chopped tomatoes
salt and ground black pepper

FOR THE MARINADE

2 red chillies, seeded and chopped
handful of fresh coriander (cilantro)
10–15ml/2–3 tsp ground cumin
15ml/1 tbsp paprika
2 garlic cloves
105ml/7 tbsp olive oil
juice of 1 lemon

1 Place all the marinade ingredients in a food processor with 5ml/1 tsp salt and blend well. Peel and devein the king prawns. Skin the fish fillets and cut into bitesize chunks, then cut the chicken into bitesize chunks. Place the fish and shellfish (except the mussels) in one bowl, and the chicken in another. Split the marinade between the two. Cover and marinate for 2 hours.

2 Scrub the mussels, discarding any that do not close when tapped. Place the rice in a large bowl, cover with boiling water and leave for 30 minutes. Strain the fish and chicken, reserving the marinade. Heat the oil in a wok. Fry the chicken until browned. Cut the courgettes into strips. Core, seed and cut the red pepper into strips. Fry the courgettes and pepper for 3–4 minutes.

3 Transfer the chicken and the vegetables to separate serving plates. Cook the marinade for 1 minute. Add the drained rice, stock, chopped tomatoes and chicken. Bring to the boil, cover and simmer for 15 minutes. Add the vegetables to the pan and top with the seafood. Cook for 12 minutes until the fish is tender and the mussels are open. Discard any mussels that have not opened. Serve hot.

Nutritional information per portion: Energy 490kcal/2056kJ; Protein 46.9g; Carbohydrate 44.1g, of which sugars 8.7g; Fat 14g, of which saturates 2g; Cholesterol 202mg; Calcium 94mg; Fibre 2.2g; Sodium 367mg.

Spicy crayfish and potato stew

This spicy dish flavoured with lashings of red-hot chilli sauce, paprika and tomatoes makes a tasty suppertime treat. The evaporated milk gives this fiery dish a delightfully creamy texture.

SERVES 6

675g/1½lb raw crayfish or king prawns (jumbo shrimp)

1kg/2¼lb floury potatoes

75ml/5 tbsp butter

1 small red onion, finely chopped

60ml/4 tbsp chilli sauce

5ml/1 tsp paprika

3 medium tomatoes, peeled, seeded and diced

5ml/1 tsp black mint or peppermint leaves, finely sliced

500g/1¼lb queso fresco or mild feta cheese, cut into 2cm/¾in dice

120ml/4fl oz/½ cup evaporated milk

15ml/1 tbsp chopped parsley or mint leaves, to garnish

salt

1 Pour 350ml/12fl oz/1½ cups water into a large pan and bring to a boil. Drop the crayfish or prawns in, cover, and cook for 10 minutes.

2 Strain and reserve the stock: there should be about 250ml/8fl oz/1 cup. Set aside six whole crayfish or prawns. Peel the rest, remove their heads, and devein.

3 Boil the potatoes in their skins in lightly salted water until tender, then, when cooled, peel them and cut into 1cm/½in slices.

4 Heat the butter in a pan and cook the onion until soft. Stir in the chilli sauce, paprika, tomatoes and mint, and cook for 3 minutes. Add the crayfish or prawn tails, the reserved stock, cheese and sliced potatoes.

5 Bring to the boil and simmer for 5 minutes, or until the cheese has melted. Add the evaporated milk, season to taste with salt and simmer for 5 more minutes. Serve, garnished with chopped parsley or mint leaves and the reserved whole crayfish or prawns.

Nutritional information per portion: Energy 541kcal/2262kJ; Protein 36.6g; Carbohydrate 34.1g, of which sugars 9.3g; Fat 29.5g, of which saturates 19g; Cholesterol 222mg; Calcium 411mg; Fibre 2.3g; Sodium 1639mg.

Lobster and crab in hot spices

Depending on the size and availability of the lobsters and crabs, you can make this delicious spicy dish for as many people as you like, because the quantities are simple to adjust.

SERVES 4

4 uncooked lobsters, about 450g/1lb each

4–8 uncooked crabs, about 225g/8oz each

about 600ml/1 pint/2¹⁄₂ cups beer

**4 spring onions (scallions), trimmed and
   chopped into long pieces**

**4cm/1¹⁄₂in fresh root ginger, peeled
   and finely sliced**

**2 green or red Thai chillies, seeded and
   finely sliced**

3 lemon grass stalks, finely sliced

1 bunch of fresh dill, fronds chopped

**1 bunch each of fresh basil and coriander
   (cilantro) leaves, chopped**

about 30ml/2 tbsp Thai fish sauce

juice of 1 lemon

salt and ground black pepper

1 Clean the lobsters and crabs well and rub them with salt and pepper. Place half of them in a steamer and pour the beer into the base.

2 Sprinkle half the spring onions, ginger, chillies, lemon grass and herbs over the lobsters and crabs, and steam for 10 minutes, or until the lobsters turn red.

3 Lift the cooked lobsters and crabs on to a serving dish, then cook the rest in the same way. Add the lemon grass, herbs and fish sauce to the simmering beer, stir in the lemon juice, then pour into a large dipping bowl.

4 Serve hot, dipping the lobster and crab meat into the broth.

Nutritional information per portion: Energy 264kcal/1112kJ; Protein 48g; Carbohydrate 4g, of which sugars 1g; Fat 7g, of which saturates 1g; Cholesterol 210mg; Calcium 185mg; Fibre 0.5g; Sodium 1.3mg.

Meat, game and poultry

Chillies crop up all over the globe, appearing in delectable dishes from places as far apart as Italy and Jamaica. This chapter features some of the best, from family favourites such as spicy meatballs and chilli con carne to dishes that would do you proud at dinner parties, such as lamb tagine and chargrilled quails.

Chilli-hot pepperoni pizza

There are few treats more tasty than a home-made freshly baked pizza. This spicy pizza is a dish that is perfect for all occasions, it can be served for supper with salads or packed for a picnic.

SERVES 4

225g/8oz/2 cups strong white
   (bread) flour
10ml/2 tsp easy-blend (rapid rise)
   dried yeast
5ml/1 tsp sugar
2.5ml/½ tsp salt
15ml/1 tbsp olive oil
175ml/6fl oz/¾ cup equal parts mixed
   hand-hot milk and water
fresh oregano leaves, to garnish

FOR THE TOPPING

400g/14oz can chopped tomatoes
2 garlic cloves, crushed
5ml/1 tsp dried oregano
225g/8oz mozzarella cheese,
   coarsely grated
2 dried red chillies
225g/8oz pepperoni, sliced
30ml/2 tbsp drained capers

1 Sift the flour into a bowl. Stir in the yeast, sugar and salt. Make a well in the centre. Stir the olive oil into the milk and water, then stir the mixture into the flour. Mix well until a soft dough forms.

2 Knead the dough on a lightly floured surface for 5–10 minutes until it is smooth and elastic in texture. Lightly oil a bowl. Place the dough in the bowl and cover with clear film (plastic wrap). Leave in a warm place for about 30 minutes or until the dough has doubled in bulk.

3 Preheat the oven to 220°C/425°F/Gas 7. Knead the dough on a lightly floured surface for 1 minute. Divide it in half and roll each piece out to a 25cm/10in circle. Place on lightly oiled pizza trays or baking sheets.

4 Make the topping. Drain the can of tomatoes in a sieve (strainer). Transfer the drained tomatoes into a bowl and stir in the crushed garlic and dried oregano. Spread half the mixture over each round, leaving a clear margin around the edge. Set half the mozzarella aside. Divide the rest between the pizzas. Bake for 7–10 minutes until the dough rim on each pizza is pale golden.

5 Crumble the chillies over the pizzas, then arrange the pepperoni slices and capers on top. Sprinkle with the reserved mozzarella. Return the pizzas to the oven and bake for 7–10 minutes more. Sprinkle over the fresh oregano and serve immediately.

Nutritional information per portion: Energy 631kcal/2640kJ; Protein 28.8g; Carbohydrate 47.6g, of which sugars 4.7g; Fat 37.6g, of which saturates 16.8g; Cholesterol 80mg; Calcium 318mg; Fibre 2.7g; Sodium 1499mg.

Baked potatoes with chilli beef

Classic chilli-flavoured beef tops crisp baked potatoes. This is a delicious and spicy meal that is very easy to prepare – perfect for a simple yet substantial family supper.

SERVES 4

2 large baking potatoes
15ml/1 tbsp vegetable oil, plus
    more for brushing
1 garlic clove, crushed
1 small onion, chopped
1/2 red (bell) pepper, chopped
225g/8oz lean minced (ground) beef
1/2 small fresh red chilli, seeded
    and chopped
5ml/1 tsp ground cumin
pinch of cayenne pepper

200g/7oz can chopped tomatoes
30ml/2 tbsp tomato paste
2.5ml/1/2 tsp fresh oregano
2.5ml/1/2 tsp fresh marjoram
200g/7oz can red kidney beans, drained
15ml/1 tbsp chopped fresh
    coriander (cilantro)
salt and ground black pepper
chopped fresh marjoram, to garnish
60ml/4 tbsp sour cream and lettuce
    leaves, to serve

1 Preheat the oven to 220°C/425°F/Gas 7. Brush or rub the potatoes with a little of the oil and then pierce them with skewers. Place the potatoes on the top shelf of the oven and bake them for 30 minutes before beginning to cook the chilli.

2 Heat the oil in a large heavy pan and add the garlic, onion and pepper. Fry gently for 4–5 minutes until softened.

3 Add the beef and fry until browned, then stir in the chilli, cumin, cayenne pepper, tomatoes, tomato paste, 60ml/4 tbsp water and the oregano. Bring to a boil then reduce the heat, cover and simmer for about 25 minutes, stirring occasionally.

4 Stir in the drained kidney beans and continue to cook uncovered for a further 5 minutes. Remove from the heat and stir in the chopped coriander. Season well and set aside.

5 Cut the baked potatoes in half and place them in serving bowls. Top the potatoes with the chilli mixture and a dollop of sour cream. Garnish with chopped fresh marjoram and serve hot accompanied by a few lettuce leaves.

Nutritional information per portion: Energy 327kcal/369kJ; Protein 17.7g; Carbohydrate 30.6g, of which sugars 8.2g; Fat 15.7g, of which saturates 6.4g; Cholesterol 43mg; Calcium 71mg; Fibre 5.2g; Sodium 277mg.

Meatballs with chilli tomato sauce

Wherever you go in Latin America, you'll find a different interpretation of this hearty family dish. Spanish in origin, the meatballs are often made with pork or veal, or a mixture of meats.

SERVES 4

500g/1¼ lb minced (ground) beef
3 garlic cloves, crushed
1 small onion, finely chopped
50g/2oz/1 cup fresh breadcrumbs
1 egg, beaten
2.5ml/½ tsp ground cumin
50g/2oz/½ cup plain (all-purpose) flour
60ml/4 tbsp olive oil
salt
cooked white rice, to serve

FOR THE SAUCE
30ml/2 tbsp olive oil
1 small onion, thinly sliced
2 red (bell) peppers, seeded and diced
2 fresh red chillies, seeded and chopped
2 garlic cloves, crushed
150ml/¼ pint/⅔ cup canned
 chopped tomatoes
400ml/14fl oz/1⅔ cups light beef stock
ground black pepper

1 Place all the beef, garlic, onion, breadcrumbs, egg and cumin in a large bowl. Using your hands, mix until thoroughly combined. Season with salt and shape the mixture into even balls. Wet your hands to prevent the mixture from sticking. Dust lightly with flour.

2 Heat the oil in a large frying pan and cook the meatballs, in batches, for 6–8 minutes or until golden. When all the meatballs have been browned, wipe the pan clean with kitchen paper.

3 To make the sauce, pour the olive oil into the pan and cook the onion and peppers over low heat for 10 minutes, until soft. Add the chillies and garlic, and cook for a further 2 minutes. Pour in the tomatoes and stock, and bring to the boil. Lower the heat, cover and simmer for 15 minutes. Season.

4 Add the meatballs to the pan and spoon the sauce over them. Bring back to the boil, then cover and simmer for 10 minutes. Serve with cooked rice.

Nutritional information per portion: Energy 335kcal/1394kJ; Protein 17.8g; Carbohydrate 11.9g, of which sugars 6.8g; Fat 24.6g, of which saturates 7.7g; Cholesterol 58mg; Calcium 45mg; Fibre 1.9g; Sodium 522mg.

Chilli beef balls

This Indonesian version of meatballs are spicy and delicious. The beef is moulded into small little balls which can be served as snacks or as an accompaniment to a cool, iced drink.

SERVES 4

5ml/1 tsp coriander seeds

5ml/1 tsp cumin seeds

175g/6oz freshly grated coconut
 or desiccated (dry unsweetened
 shredded) coconut

15ml/1 tbsp coconut oil

4 shallots, finely chopped

2 garlic cloves, finely chopped

1–2 red chillies, seeded and
 finely chopped

350g/12oz minced (ground) beef

beaten egg (if necessary)

rice flour, to coat

corn oil, for shallow-frying

salt and ground black pepper

1 lime, quartered, and plum sauce
 to serve

1 In a pan, dry-fry the coriander and cumin seeds until they give off a nutty aroma. Using a mortar and pestle, grind the roasted seeds to a powder.

2 In the same pan, dry-fry the grated coconut until it begins to colour. Transfer the coconut on to a plate and leave to cool. Heat the coconut oil, stir in the shallots, garlic and chillies and fry until they colour. Transfer to a plate.

3 Put the beef into a bowl and add the ground spices, dry-fried coconut and shallot mixture. Season with salt and pepper. Bind all the ingredients together, adding a little egg if necessary. Knead the mixture and mould it into little balls, then coat the balls in rice flour.

4 Heat a thin layer of corn oil in a frying pan and fry the meatballs for about 5 minutes until they are golden brown. Drain then arrange on a serving dish. Serve with the lime wedges and the plum sauce.

Nutritional information per portion: Energy 559kcal/2312kJ; Protein 20.2g; Carbohydrate 8g, of which sugars 3.7g; Fat 49.6g, of which saturates 30.4g; Cholesterol 53mg; Calcium 23mg; Fibre 6.3g; Sodium 83mg.

Chilli con carne

This classic Tex-Mex stew has become a favourite all around the world. Serve it with rice or baked potatoes and a hearty green salad. Garnish with sliced red chillies for extra fire.

SERVES 8

1.2kg/2¹/₂lb lean braising steak
2 large onions
2 garlic cloves
30ml/2 tbsp sunflower oil
15ml/1 tbsp plain (all-purpose) flour
300ml/¹/₂ pint/1¹/₄ cups red wine
300ml/¹/₂ pint/1¹/₄ cups beef stock
30ml/2 tbsp tomato purée (paste)
30ml/2 tbsp olive oil
1 fresh red chilli, seeded and chopped
2 x 400g/14oz cans red kidney beans,
   drained and rinsed

400g/14oz can chopped tomatoes
6 fresh tomatoes, peeled and chopped
1 fresh green chilli, seeded
   and chopped
30ml/2 tbsp chopped fresh chives
30ml/2 tbsp chopped fresh coriander
   (cilantro), plus sprigs to garnish
150ml/¹/₄ pint/²/₃ cup sour cream
salt and ground black pepper
cooked rice, to serve

1 Cut the beef into thick strips, then cut it crossways into small cubes. Place the beef cubes on to a plate and keep to one side. Peel the onions and garlic and finely chop.

2 Heat the sunflower oil in a large, flameproof casserole. Add the garlic and half of the chopped onion, and cook until they are softened but not coloured.

3 Place the plain flour in a large bowl or plate. Season the flour with salt and black pepper. Toss a batch of beef cubes in it, making sure the beef is coated well in the flour.

4 Use a slotted spoon to remove the cooked onion from the pan, then add the floured beef and cook over high heat until the meat is browned on all sides. Remove the cooked beef from the pan and set aside, then flour and brown another batch of the beef cubes. Continue to do this until all the beef has been browned.

5 When the last batch of beef has been browned, return the cooked onion and garlic to the pan. Stir in the red wine, beef stock and the tomato purée. Bring to the boil, reduce the heat and simmer for 45 minutes, or until the beef is tender.

6 Meanwhile, heat the olive oil in a frying pan and cook the rest of the chopped onion and red chilli until softened. Stir in the kidney beans and the can of chopped tomatoes, and simmer gently for 20–25 minutes, or until the bean mixture has thickened and reduced.

7 Ladle the beef mixture on to warmed bowls. Add a layer of bean mixture. Mix the chopped fresh tomatoes, green chilli, chives and coriander together and place on top of the beef and bean mixture. Serve with cooked rice, and top with sour cream and garnish with coriander leaves.

Nutritional information per portion: Energy 289cal/1216kJ; Protein 27.3g; Carbohydrate 24.7g, of which sugars 7.9g; Fat 9.7g, of which saturates 2.8g; Cholesterol 45mg; Calcium 61mg; Fibre7.8g; Sodium 65mg.

Beef with jalapeño chillies

Fine strips of braised beef are enhanced by a rich, dark soy and garlic sauce, with a piquant kick of root ginger. Muscovado sugar adds sweetness, complemented by hot jalapeño chillies.

SERVES 3–4

450g/1lb beef frying (flank) steak
25g/1oz fresh root ginger
100ml/3¹/₂fl oz/scant ¹/₂ cup
   dark soy sauce
75g/3oz light muscovado
   (brown) sugar
12 garlic cloves, peeled
6 jalapeño chillies

1 Bring a large pan of water to the boil and add the beef. Cook for around 40 minutes until tender. Drain the meat and rinse it in warm water. Leave the beef to cool, then roughly slice it into strips about 5cm/2in long.

2 Peel the root ginger and place it in a large pan with the cooked beef and add 300ml/¹/₂ pint/1¹/₄ cups water. Bring to the boil, cover, then reduce the heat and simmer for 30 minutes. Skim the fat from the surface of the liquid as the meat cooks. The liquid should have reduced to half its initial volume.

3 Add the soy sauce, muscovado sugar and garlic, and simmer for a further 20 minutes. Then add the jalapeño chillies, and cook for a further 5 minutes.

4 Discard the root ginger from the pan, and serve the beef strips in warmed bowls with the garlic cloves and jalapeño chillies.

Nutritional information per portion: Energy 657kcal/2730kJ; Protein 41.4g; Carbohydrate 25.1g, of which sugars 24.9g; Fat 43.5g, of which saturates 10g; Cholesterol 94mg; Calcium 231mg; Fibre 4.5g; Sodium 504mg.

Chilli beef pie

This dish is similar to a classic lasagne, except that the beef is mixed with lots of fresh chillies and rice which is layered between tortillas, and finished off with a super-hot salsa sauce.

SERVES 8

3 fresh red chillies, seeded and sliced
2 x 400g/14oz cans chopped tomatoes
4 garlic cloves, crushed
2 onions, chopped
5ml/1 tsp ground cumin
2.5–5ml/¹/₂–1 tsp cayenne pepper
2.5ml/¹/₂ tsp dried oregano
50g/2oz/4 tbsp butter
50g/2oz/¹/₂ cup plain (all-purpose) flour
600ml/1 pint/2¹/₂ cups milk
115g/4oz/1 cup grated Cheddar cheese
350g/12oz rump (round) steak, cubed
15ml/1 tbsp oil
225g/8oz/2 cups cooked rice
beef stock, to moisten
3 large wheat tortillas
salt and ground black pepper

1 Preheat the oven to 180°C/350°F/Gas 4. To make the salsa, place 1 red chilli, the tomatoes, half the garlic, half the onion in a blender or food processor and process until smooth. Transfer to a small pan. Add the cumin, cayenne pepper and oregano and season. Bring to the boil, and cook for 1–2 minutes, then cover and simmer for 15 minutes. Set aside.

2 To make the cheese sauce, melt the butter and stir in the flour. Cook for 1 minute. Add the milk and cook until it thickens. Stir in all but 30ml/2 tbsp of the cheese and season. Set aside.

3 Mix the remaining onion, garlic and chillies in a bowl. Add the beef and mix well. Heat the oil in a frying pan and stir-fry the mixture for 10 minutes.

4 Stir in the rice and beef stock. Season. Pour a quarter of the cheese sauce into an ovenproof dish. Add a tortilla. Spread over half the salsa, then half the meat. Repeat these layers for all the tortillas. Then pour over the last of the sauce and sprinkle on the reserved cheese. Bake for 15–20 minutes.

Nutritional information per portion: Energy 595kcal/2516kJ; Protein 30.3g; Carbohydrate 91.2g, of which sugars 11.3g; Fat 14.7g, of which saturates 4.7g; Cholesterol 53mg; Calcium 153mg; Fibre 4.0g; Sodium 379mg.

Spicy pumpkin and beef stew

This colourful stew is a prime example of Argentinian cooking. The tender beef cooked with fresh chillies and red wine balances the sweetness of the peaches, potatoes and pumpkin.

SERVES 6–8

1 large pumpkin, about 5kg/11lb
60ml/4 tbsp olive oil
1kg/2¼lb braising steak, cut into
    2.5cm/1in cubes
1 large onion, finely chopped
3 fresh red chillies, seeded and chopped
2 garlic cloves, crushed
1 large tomato, roughly chopped
2 fresh bay leaves
600ml/1 pint/2½ cups beef stock

350ml/12fl oz/1½ cups red wine
500g/1¼lb potatoes, peeled and cut into
    2cm/¾in cubes
500g/1¼lb sweet potatoes, peeled and
    cut into 2cm/¾in cubes
1 corn cob, cut widthways into
    6 slices
3 peaches, peeled, stoned (pitted) and cut
    into thick wedges
salt and ground black pepper

1 Wash the outside of the pumpkin. Using a sharp knife, carefully cut a slice off the top 6cm/2½in from the stem, to make a lid. Using a spoon, scoop out the seeds and stringy fibres and discard. Scoop out some of the flesh, leaving a shell about 2cm/¾in thick inside of the pumpkin. Cut the flesh you have removed into 1cm/½in pieces.

2 Brush the inside of the pumpkin and the flesh side of the lid with a little olive oil. Season with salt and ground black pepper. Place both pumpkin and lid on a baking sheet, flesh side up. Set aside.

3 Preheat the oven to 200°C/400°F/Gas 6. Heat half the remaining olive oil in a large heavy pan over high heat. Add the beef, season and sauté for 8–10 minutes, until golden brown, then remove with a slotted spoon – you may need to do this in batches. Avoid adding too much beef to the pan or it will steam rather than brown.

4 Lower the heat and add the remaining oil to the pan. Stir in the onion and chillies, and sauté for 5 minutes. Scrape the base of the pan with a wooden spoon, to loosen any sediment. Add the garlic and tomato and cook for 2 minutes more.

5 Return the meat to the pan and add the bay leaves, stock and red wine. Bring to the boil, then lower the heat to a gentle simmer. Cook for 1 hour or until the meat is tender.

6 Place the baking sheet containing the pumpkin and its lid in the oven and bake for 30 minutes.

7 Add the potatoes, sweet potatoes, pieces of pumpkin and corn to the stew. Pour in more liquid if needed and bring to the boil. Reduce the heat to a simmer, cover and cook for 15 minutes.

8 Finally add the peach wedges and season with salt and black pepper to taste. Spoon the stew into the partially cooked pumpkin shell, cover with the pumpkin lid and bake for 15 minutes.

9 Carefully lift the filled pumpkin shell on to a large, strong platter and take it to the table. Ladle the hot stew on to bowls, then cut the empty pumpkin into six to eight wedges, depending on the number of people to be served.

Nutritional information per portion: Energy 483kcal/2028kJ; Protein 34.2g; Carbohydrate 39.8g, of which sugars 16.8g; Fat 18.6g, of which saturates 6.1g; Cholesterol 73mg; Calcium 151mg; Fibre 7.4g; Sodium 120mg.

Chilli beef enchiladas

Dried chillies are a wonderful pantry staple. It is worth having a supply of several different types, so you'll always have the means to make spicy dishes like this one.

SERVES 3–4

500g/1¼ lb rump (round) steak,
   cut into 5cm/2in cubes
2 ancho chillies, seeded
2 pasilla chillies, seeded
2 garlic cloves, crushed
10ml/2 tsp dried oregano
2.5ml/½ tsp ground cumin
30ml/2 tbsp vegetable oil
7 fresh corn tortillas
shredded onion and flat leaf
   parsley, to garnish
salsa, to serve

1 Put the steak in a deep frying pan and cover with water. Bring to the boil, then lower the heat and simmer for 1–1½ hours, or until very tender.

2 Meanwhile, put the dried chillies in a bowl and pour over the hot water. Leave to soak for 30 minutes, then transfer the contents of the bowl into a blender and blend to a smooth paste.

3 Drain the steak and let it cool, reserving 250ml/8fl oz/1 cup of the cooking liquid. Fry the garlic, oregano and cumin in the oil for 2 minutes. Stir in the chilli paste and the reserved cooking liquid.

4 Tear one of the tortillas into small pieces and add it to the mixture. Bring to the boil, then simmer. Simmer for 10 minutes, stirring occasionally, until thickened. Shred the steak and stir it into the sauce and heat. Wrap the tortillas and steam on a plate over boiling water until pliable. Divide the meat mixture between the tortillas and roll them up to make enchiladas. Garnish with shreds of onion and parsley and serve with the salsa.

Nutritional information per portion: Energy 460kcal/1939kJ; Protein 38g; Carbohydrate 52.4g, of which sugars 1.1g; Fat 12.3g, of which saturates 3.1g; Cholesterol 84mg; Calcium 108mg; Fibre 2.1g; Sodium 331mg.

Lamb meatballs with chilli tomato sauce

Serve these piquant chilli-flavoured Italian-style meatballs with pasta and a leafy salad. Sprinkle with a little grated Parmesan cheese for that extra Italian touch.

SERVES 4

450g/1lb lean minced (ground) lamb
1 large onion, grated
1 garlic clove, crushed
50g/2oz/1 cup fresh white breadcrumbs
15ml/1 tbsp chopped fresh parsley
1 small egg, lightly beaten
30ml/2 tbsp olive oil
salt and ground black pepper
Parmesan cheese, pasta and rocket
   (arugula) leaves, to serve

FOR THE SAUCE

1 onion, finely chopped
400g/14oz can chopped tomatoes
200ml/7fl oz/scant 1 cup passata
   (bottled strained tomatoes)
5ml/1 tsp sugar
2 green chillies, seeded and
   finely chopped
30ml/2 tbsp chopped fresh oregano
salt and ground black pepper

1 Soak a small clay pot in cold water for 15 minutes, then drain. Place the minced lamb, onion, garlic, breadcrumbs, parsley and seasoning in a bowl and mix well. Add the beaten egg and mix to bind the meatball mixture together.

2 Roll the mixture in your hands and shape into about 20 even balls, about the size of walnuts. Wetting your hands slightly will prevent the mixture sticking to them. Heat the olive oil in a frying pan, add the meatballs and cook over high heat, stirring occasionally, until browned all over.

3 Meanwhile, to make the sauce, mix together the chopped onion, tomatoes, passata, sugar, seeded and chopped chillies and oregano in a large bowl. Season well with salt and pepper and pour the sauce into the clay pot.

4 Place the meatballs in the sauce, then cover and place in an oven. Set the oven to 200°C/400°F/Gas 6 and cook for 1 hour, stirring after 30 minutes.

5 Serve the meatballs over cooked pasta with a sprinkling of grated Parmesan cheese on top. Garnish with fresh rocket leaves.

Nutritional information per portion: Energy 443kcal/1853kJ; Protein 33.1g; Carbohydrate 22.5g, of which sugars 11.1g; Fat 25.3g, of which saturates 10.3g; Cholesterol 148mg; Calcium 246mg; Fibre 3g; Sodium 389mg.

Chargrilled chilli lamb kebabs

This is the ultimate kebab: spicy chargrilled meat served on a pide, a Turkish flat bread, with yogurt and tomatoes. Topped with a chilli sauce, this one really does hit the hot spot.

SERVES 4

12 plum tomatoes
30ml/2 tbsp butter
1 large pide, or 4 pitta or small naan
5ml/1 tsp ground sumac
5ml/1 tsp dried oregano
225g/8oz/1 cup natural (plain) yogurt
salt and ground black pepper
1 bunch fresh flat leaf parsley, chopped

FOR THE KEBABS
500g/1¼lb minced (ground) lamb
2 onions, finely chopped
1 green chilli, seeded and chopped

4 garlic cloves, crushed
5ml/1 tsp Turkish red pepper or paprika
5ml/1 tsp ground sumac
1 bunch flat leaf parsley, chopped

FOR THE SAUCE
30ml/2 tbsp olive oil
15ml/1 tbsp butter
1 onion, finely chopped
2 garlic cloves, finely chopped
1 green chilli, seeded and chopped
5–10ml/1–2 tsp sugar
400g/14oz can chopped tomato

1 Make the kebabs. Put the lamb and other ingredients in a bowl and knead to a paste. Cover and chill for 15 minutes.

2 Make the sauce. Heat the oil and butter in a pan, stir in the onion, garlic and chilli and cook until they colour. Add the sugar and tomatoes and cook for 30 minutes. Season and set aside.

3 Light the barbecue and shape the kebabs. Cook on the barbecue for 6–8 minutes, turning once. Meanwhile, thread the tomatoes on to skewers and cook on the barbecue until charred.

4 While the kebabs are cooking, melt the butter in a heavy pan. Cut the pide, pitta or naan into bitesize chunks and fry until golden. Sprinkle with sumac and oregano, then arrange on a serving dish. Splash a little sauce over the bread and spoon half the yogurt on top.

5 Cut the kebab meat into bitesize pieces. Arrange on the bread with the tomatoes, sprinkle with salt and the rest of the sumac and oregano, and garnish with the chopped parsley. Serve hot, topped with dollops of the remaining sauce and yogurt.

Nutritional information per portion: Energy 642kcal/2688kJ; Protein 35.2g; Carbohydrate 52.8g, of which sugars 24.1g; Fat 33.9g, of which saturates 15.1g; Cholesterol 121mg; Calcium 253mg; Fibre 6.3g; Sodium 456mg.

Spicy lamb tagine

In this warming Moroccan dish, lamb meatballs are poached gently with lemon and hot spices to make a delicious meal that is quite light. Serve it with a salad, plain couscous or crusty bread.

SERVES 4

450g/1lb finely minced (ground) lamb

3 large onions, grated

small bunch of flat leaf parsley, chopped

5–10ml/1–2 tsp ground cinnamon

5ml/1 tsp ground cumin

pinch of cayenne pepper

40g/1¹/₂oz/3 tbsp butter

25g/1oz fresh root ginger, peeled and
    finely chopped

1 chilli, seeded and finely chopped

pinch of saffron threads

small bunch of fresh coriander (cilantro),
    finely chopped

juice of 1 lemon

300ml/¹/₂ pint/1¹/₄ cups water

1 lemon, quartered

salt and ground black pepper

crusty bread, to serve

1 To make the meatballs, pound the minced lamb in a bowl by using your hand to lift it up and slap it back down into the bowl. Knead in half the grated onions, the parsley, cinnamon, cumin and cayenne pepper.

2 Season with salt and pepper, and continue pounding the mixture by hand for a few minutes. Break off pieces and shape them into walnut-size balls.

3 In a heavy-lidded frying pan, melt the butter and add the remaining onion with the ginger, chilli and saffron. Stirring frequently, cook just until the onion begins to colour, then stir in the coriander and lemon juice.

4 Pour in the water, season with salt and bring to the boil. Drop in the meatballs, reduce the heat and cover the pan. Poach the meatballs gently, turning them occasionally, for about 20 minutes.

5 Remove the lid, tuck the lemon quarters around the meatballs and cook, uncovered, for a further 10 minutes to reduce the liquid slightly. Serve hot, straight from the pan with lots of crusty fresh bread to mop up the delicious juices.

Nutritional information per portion: Energy 362kcal/1503kJ; Protein 424.5g; Carbohydrate 12.9g, of which sugars 9.3g; Fat 24g, of which saturates 12.2g; Cholesterol 108mg; Calcium 134mg; Fibre 4g; Sodium 155mg.

Lamb stew with chilli sauce

The fiery guajillo and pasilla chillies in this stew add depth and richness to the sauce, while the potato slices ensure that it is substantial enough to serve on its own.

SERVES 6

6 guajillo chillies, seeded

2 pasilla chillies, seeded

250ml/8fl oz/1 cup hot water

3 garlic cloves, peeled

5ml/1 tsp ground cinnamon

2.5ml/½ tsp ground cloves

2.5ml/½ tsp ground black pepper

15ml/1 tbsp vegetable oil

1kg/2¼lb lean boneless lamb shoulder,
    cut into 2cm/¾in cubes

400g/14oz potatoes, scrubbed and
    cut into 1cm/½in thick slices

salt

strips of red (bell) pepper and fresh
    oregano to garnish

cooked rice, to serve

1 Snap or tear the dried chillies into large pieces, put them in a bowl and pour over the hot water. Leave them to soak for 30 minutes, then transfer into a food processor or blender. Add the garlic, cinnamon, cloves and black pepper. Process the mixture to a smooth paste.

2 Heat the oil in a large pan. Add the lamb cubes, in batches, and stir-fry over high heat until the cubes are evenly browned on all sides. Return all the lamb cubes to the pan, spread them out, then cover them with a layer of potato slices. Add salt to taste. Put a lid on the pan and cook over medium heat for about 10 minutes.

3 Pour over the chilli mixture and mix well. Replace the lid then simmer over low heat for about 1 hour, or until the meat and the potatoes are tender. Serve with rice, and garnish with strips of red pepper and oregano.

Nutritional information per portion: Energy 367kcal/1536kJ; Protein 34g; Carbohydrate 11.8g, of which sugars 1.9g; Fat 20.8g, of which saturates 9g; Cholesterol 127mg; Calcium 19mg; Fibre 0.9g; Sodium 151mg.

Fried rabbit with chilli

A traditional Spanish dish where the meat is marinated in wine and vinegar and then sizzled in red-hot spices and simmered in its sauces. Serve with fried potatoes for a delicious meal.

SERVES 4

675g/1½lb rabbit, jointed
300ml/½ pint/1¼ cups dry
   white wine
15ml/1 tbsp sherry vinegar
several oregano sprigs
2 bay leaves
30ml/2 tbsp plain (all-purpose) flour
90ml/6 tbsp olive oil
175g/6oz baby (pearl) onions, peeled
   and left whole
4 garlic cloves, sliced
150ml/¼ pint/⅔ cup chicken stock
1 dried chilli, seeded and finely chopped
10ml/2 tsp paprika
salt and ground black pepper

1 Put the rabbit in a bowl. Add the wine, vinegar, oregano and bay leaves and toss together. Marinate overnight in the refrigerator.

2 Drain the rabbit, reserving the marinade, and pat it dry with kitchen paper. Season the flour and use to dust the marinated rabbit.

3 Heat the oil in a flameproof casserole or frying pan. Fry the rabbit pieces until golden, then remove them and set aside. Fry the onions until they colour, and set aside. Add the garlic to the pan and continue to fry, then add the strained marinade, with the chicken stock, chilli and paprika.

4 Return the rabbit and the reserved onions to the pan. Bring to a simmer, then cover and simmer gently for about 45 minutes until the rabbit is tender. Check the seasoning, adding more vinegar and paprika if necessary. Divide among four warmed serving bowls and serve hot.

Nutritional information per portion: Energy 311kcal/1294kJ; Protein 23.2g; Carbohydrate 9.5g, of which sugars 2.6g; Fat 20.4g, of which saturates 4.1g; Cholesterol 83mg; Calcium 65mg; Fibre 0.9g; Sodium 52mg.

Venison chops with romesco sauce

Romesco is the Catalan word for the ñora chilli. It lends a spicy roundness to one of Spain's hottest sauces. It can be served cold as a dip, but this version is the ideal partner for game chops.

SERVES 4

4 venison chops, cut 2cm/³⁄₄in thick and
    about 175–200g/6–7oz each
30ml/2 tbsp olive oil
50g/2oz/4 tbsp butter
braised Savoy cabbage, to serve

FOR THE SAUCE
3 ñora chillies
1 hot dried chilli

25g/1oz/¹⁄₄ cup almonds
150ml/¹⁄₄ pint/²⁄₃ cup olive oil
1 slice stale bread, crusts removed
3 garlic cloves, chopped
3 tomatoes, peeled, seeded and
    roughly chopped
60ml/4 tbsp sherry vinegar
60ml/4 tbsp red wine vinegar
salt and ground black pepper

1 To make the romesco sauce, slit the chillies and remove the seeds, then leave the chillies to soak in warm water for 30 minutes until soft. Drain the chillies, dry them on kitchen paper and chop finely.

2 Dry-fry the almonds in a frying pan over medium heat, shaking the pan occasionally, until the nuts are toasted evenly. Transfer the nuts to a food processor or blender.

3 Add 45ml/3 tbsp oil to the pan and fry the bread slice until golden on both sides. Lift it out with a slotted spoon and drain on kitchen paper. Tear the bread and add to the food processor or blender. Fry the garlic in the remaining oil.

4 Add the soaked chillies and tomatoes to the processor or blender. Add in the garlic, with the oil from the pan and blend the mixture to form a smooth paste. With the motor running, gradually add the remaining olive oil and then the sherry and wine vinegars. When the sauce is smooth, scrape it into a bowl and season to taste. Cover with clear film (plastic wrap) and chill for 2 hours.

5 Season the chops with pepper. Heat the olive oil and butter in a heavy frying pan and fry the chops for about 5 minutes each side until golden brown and cooked through. When the chops are almost cooked, transfer the sauce to a pan and heat it gently. If it is too thick, stir in a little boiling water. Serve the sauce with the chops, accompanied by braised cabbage.

Nutritional information per portion: Energy 415kcal/1741kJ; Protein 46.9g; Carbohydrate 6.2g, of which sugars 2.9g; Fat 24g, of which saturates 9.3g; Cholesterol 127mg; Calcium 40mg; Fibre 1.3g; Sodium 229mg.

Wild boar cacciatora

A pinch of dried chilli adds a gentle warmth to this deliciously rustic Italian wild boar stew. Marinating the meat overnight makes it extremely tender. Serve with greens, such as spinach.

SERVES 4

45ml/3 tbsp extra virgin olive oil
2 onions, thickly sliced
2 celery sticks, thickly sliced
2 carrots, thickly sliced
900g/2lb wild boar meat
about 500ml/17fl oz/2¼ cups
   dry red wine
1 large rosemary sprig
cooked spinach, to serve

FOR THE CACCIATORA SAUCE

200g/7oz can tomatoes
1 onion, chopped
1 small carrot, quartered
1 small parsley sprig
5 fresh basil leaves
75ml/5 tbsp extra virgin olive oil
1 garlic clove, crushed
1 dried red chilli
sea salt

1 To make the cacciatora sauce, put the tomatoes, half the onion, carrot, parsley and basil leaves in a large pan, cover and bring to the boil, then simmer for 30 minutes. Add the oil to a frying pan with the garlic, the remaining onion and the dried chilli. Fry together for 5 minutes, stirring, then pour in the tomato sauce. Season with salt and simmer gently for 10 minutes.

2 Meanwhile, put the olive oil in a large pan and fry the onions, celery and carrots for about 10–15 minutes, or until well browned.

3 Cut the wild boar into large chunks and place in a bowl. Pour in the wine and add the rosemary and then the vegetables. The wine should cover the meat completely; add more wine if necessary and mix everything together with your hands. Leave the meat to marinate overnight.

4 Drain and dry the meat, reserving the marinade. In a wide, preferably non-stick, pan, brown all the meat so that it releases its juices, then remove from the heat and set it aside. Discard the liquid left in the pan.

5 Add the meat to the sauce. Lower the heat, cover and simmer for 1 hour, or until the meat is tender. Add some more of the marinade if the meat appears to be drying out while simmering. Serve with the cooked spinach.

Nutritional information per portion: Energy 430kcal/1791kJ; Protein 33.8g; Carbohydrate 7.5g, of which sugars 4.7g; Fat 23.5g, of which saturates 5.1g; Cholesterol 100mg; Calcium 39mg; Fibre 1.5g; Sodium 294mg.

Pork meatballs with chipotle chilli sauce

This tasty meatball dish is hard to beat and is a great introduction to the charm of chillies. The chipotle chilli gives the sauce a distinctive and slightly smoky flavour.

SERVES 4

225g/8oz minced (ground) pork
225g/8oz lean minced (ground) beef
2 onions, finely chopped
50g/2oz/1 cup fresh white breadcrumbs
5ml/1 tsp dried oregano
2.5ml/^{1}/$_2$ tsp ground cumin
2.5ml/^{1}/$_2$ tsp salt
2.5ml/^{1}/$_2$ tsp ground black pepper
1 egg, beaten
1 chipotle chilli, seeded
15ml/1 tbsp vegetable oil
2 garlic cloves, crushed
175ml/6fl oz/^{3}/$_4$ cup beef stock
400g/14oz can chopped tomatoes
105ml/7 tbsp passata (bottled
    strained tomatoes)
vegetable oil, for frying
fresh oregano sprigs, to garnish
cooked rice, to serve

1 Mix the minced pork and beef in a bowl. Add the half the chopped onion, breadcrumbs, oregano, cumin, salt and pepper. Mix well. Stir in the egg, mix well, then roll into 4cm/1^1/$_2$in balls. Put these on a baking sheet and chill.

2 Soak the chipotle chilli in hot water for 15 minutes. Heat the oil in a pan and fry the remaining onion and the garlic for 3–4 minutes until soft. Drain the chilli, reserving the soaking water, then chop and add to the mixture.

3 Fry for 1 minute, then stir in the beef stock, tomatoes, passata and soaking water. Season. Bring to the boil, and then simmer, stirring occasionally.

4 Heat the vegetable oil in a frying pan and fry the meatballs in batches for about 5 minutes, turning occasionally, until browned. Drain off the oil and transfer to a dish. Pour over the sauce and simmer for 10 minutes, stirring occasionally so that the meatballs are coated well. Transfer to serving plates, garnish with the oregano and serve with boiled rice.

Nutritional information per portion: Energy 412kcal/1717kJ; Protein 26.2g; Carbohydrate 16g, of which sugars 5.9g; Fat 27.6g, of which saturates 7.7g; Cholesterol 118mg; Calcium 50mg; Fibre 1.9g; Sodium 265mg.

Pork ribs in chilli black bean sauce

Black bean sauce goes particularly well with pork. In this extra spicy version, boiling the ribs first ensures a more succulent texture and better absorption of the chilli seasonings.

SERVES 4

8 large meaty pork spare ribs
500ml/17fl oz/generous 2 cups water
30ml/2 tbsp light soy sauce
15g/1/2oz fresh root ginger
3 garlic cloves
2 red chillies
45ml/3 tbsp sesame oil
30ml/2 tbsp black bean sauce
lime wedges, to serve

1 Cut each rib into 6cm/2^1/2in pieces. Fill a wok or a large heavy pan with water. Add the light soy sauce and bring to the boil. Add the ribs and cook in the boiling water for 20 minutes. Drain, reserving the stock for another dish.

2 Finely chop the ginger, garlic and chillies. Blend the sesame oil with the black bean sauce and add the ginger, garlic and chillies.

3 Place the cooked ribs in a shallow dish and pour the mixture over, then leave to marinate for at least several hours or overnight. When you are ready to cook, lift the ribs out of the marinade and arrange them in a shallow dish.

4 Put the dish in a steamer, cover and steam the ribs for about 15 minutes until they are heated through and tender. Serve with the lime wedges.

Nutritional information per portion: Energy 722Kcal/3012kJ; Protein 61.8g; Carbohydrate 2.6g, of which sugars 1g; Fat 51.9g, of which saturates 18.1g; Cholesterol 215mg; Calcium 59mg; Fibre 0.7g; Sodium 897mg.

Pork chops in a spicy sauce

These sizzling pork chops are great favourites with everyone. There are four red chillies in the sauce so be prepared for a fiery flavour. If you want it even hotter, include the chilli seeds.

SERVES 4

4 pork chops
4 large mushrooms
4 fresh red chillies
30ml/2 tbsp spring onions (scallions)
45ml/3 tbsp vegetable oil
45ml/3 tbsp Thai fish sauce
90ml/6 tbsp fresh lime juice
4 shallots, chopped
5ml/1 tsp roasted ground rice
tagliatelle, cooked, to serve

FOR THE MARINADE

2 garlic cloves, chopped
15ml/1 tbsp sugar
15ml/1 tbsp Thai fish sauce
30ml/2 tbsp soy sauce
15ml/1 tbsp sesame oil
15ml/1 tbsp whisky or dry sherry
2 lemon grass stalks, finely chopped
2 spring onions (scallions), chopped

1 Make the marinade. Combine all the ingredients in a large dish.

2 Add the pork chops, coating them in the marinade. Cover and leave to marinate for 1–2 hours. Lift the chops out of the marinade and place them on a grill (broiler) rack.

3 Brush the pork chops with the marinade and cook for 5–7 minutes on each side. Brush the mushrooms with the marinade and cook for about 2 minutes.

4 Chop and deseed the chillies, and chop the spring onions.

5 Heat the remaining oil in a wok or frying pan, then remove the pan from the heat and stir in the chillies, fish sauce, lime juice, shallots, ground rice and spring onions.

6 Divide the cooked tagliatelle among four individual serving plates, and place the pork chops and mushrooms on top and spoon over the sauce. Serve hot.

Nutritional information per portion: Energy 339kcal/1418kJ; Protein 39.7g; Carbohydrate 2.3g, of which sugars 1g; Fat 19.1g, of which saturates 4.1g; Cholesterol 90mg; Calcium 26mg; Fibre 1g; Sodium 678mg.

Chilli pork with chickpeas and orange

The orange gives a sweetness to this super spicy stew. All you need to serve with this fiery dish is fresh, crusty bread to mop up the juices and a simple bowl of black olives.

SERVES 4

350g/12oz/1³/₄ cups dried chickpeas, soaked overnight in water to cover
75–90ml/5–6 tbsp olive oil
675g/1¹/₂lb boneless leg of pork, cut into large cubes
1 large onion, sliced
2 garlic cloves, chopped
400g/14oz can chopped tomatoes
grated rind of 1 orange
1 small dried red chilli
salt and ground black pepper

1 Drain the chickpeas, rinse them under cold water and drain. Place in a large pan. Pour in enough cold water to cover generously, put a lid on the pan and bring to the boil.

2 Cover and cook gently for 1–1¹/₂ hours. When the chickpeas are soft, drain them, reserving the cooking liquid, and set them aside.

3 Heat the olive oil in a pan and brown the meat in batches. Transfer the pork cubes to a plate as they brown. When the meat is done, add the onion to the oil remaining in the pan and fry until golden.

4 Add the chopped garlic, then add the tomatoes and orange rind. Crumble in the dried red chilli. Return the chickpeas and meat to the pan, and pour in enough of the reserved cooking liquid to cover. Add the black pepper, but not salt at this stage.

5 Mix well, cover the pan and simmer for 1 hour, or until the meat is tender. Stir occasionally and add more of the reserved liquid if needed. The result should be a moist casserole; not soupy, but not dry either. Season to taste with salt and serve immediately.

Nutritional information per portion: Energy 663kcal/2,781kJ; Protein 56.7g; Carbohydrate 54.4g, of which sugars 11g; Fat 25.7g, of which saturates 4.9g; Cholesterol 106mg; Calcium 184mg; Fibre 11.8g; Sodium 164mg.

Spicy pork stir-fry

This simple dish is easy to prepare. The potent flavour of chilli paste predominates in the fabulously spicy seasoning for the thinly sliced pork and will set the tastebuds aflame. Serve with rice to help counterbalance the fiery character of the dish.

SERVES 2

400g/14oz pork shoulder
1 onion
1/2 carrot
2 spring onions (scallions)
15ml/1 tbsp vegetable oil
1/2 red chilli, finely sliced
1/2 green chilli, finely sliced
steamed rice and miso soup,
   to serve

FOR THE SEASONING

30ml/2 tbsp dark soy sauce
30ml/2 tbsp chilli paste
30ml/2 tbsp mirin or rice wine
15ml/1 tbsp chilli powder
1 garlic clove, finely chopped
1 spring onion (scallion), finely chopped
15ml/1 tbsp grated fresh root ginger
15ml/1 tbsp sesame oil
30ml/2 tbsp sugar
ground black pepper

1 Place the pork shoulder in the freezer and freeze for 30 minutes, to make slicing easier. Once chilled, slice it thinly, to about 5mm/1/4in thick. Cut the onion and carrot into thin strips, and slice the spring onions into lengthways strips, reserving some to garnish.

2 To make the seasoning, combine the seasoning ingredients in a large bowl, mixing together thoroughly to form a paste. If the mixture looks too dry, add a splash of water to moisten.

3 Heat a wok or large frying pan, and add the vegetable oil. Once the oil is smoking, add the pork, onion, carrot, spring onions and chillies. Stir-fry the ingredients, ensuring that they are kept moving all the time in the pan.

4 Once the pork has lightly browned, add the seasoning, and thoroughly coat the meat and vegetables. Stir-fry for 2 minutes more, or until the pork is cooked through.

5 Garnish with the reserved strips of spring onion, and serve with rice and a bowl of miso soup to help balance the spicy flavours of the dish.

Nutritional information per portion: Energy 430kcal/1799kJ; Protein 44.1g; Carbohydrate 21.3g, of which sugars 20.4g; Fat 19.2g, of which saturates 4.3g; Cholesterol 126mg; Calcium 44mg; Fibre 1.2g; Sodium 1216mg.

Spicy pork curry

This super-hot curry can be made with butternut squash, pumpkin or winter melon, and is flavoured with fresh chillies. Serve this delicious dish with rice and bread to mop up the sauce.

SERVES 3–4

2 red Thai chillies
3 shallots, halved and finely sliced
30ml/2 tbsp groundnut (peanut) oil
25g/1oz galangal, finely sliced
30ml/2 tbsp kroeung
10ml/2 tsp ground turmeric
5ml/1 tsp ground fenugreek
10ml/2 tsp palm sugar (jaggery)
450g/1lb pork loin, cut into small chunks
30ml/2 tbsp Thai fish sauce
900ml/1½ pints/3¾ cups coconut milk
1 butternut squash, peeled, seeded and
    cut into bitesize chunks
4 kaffir lime leaves
sea salt and ground black pepper
1 small bunch fresh coriander (cilantro),
    coarsely chopped and 1 small bunch
    fresh mint, stalks removed, to garnish
plain rice or noodles and salad, to serve

1 Peel the chillies and cut them in half. Carefully scrape out the seeds and finely slice. Peel, halve and finely slice the shallots.

2 Heat the oil in a work or a large heavy pan. Stir in the galangal, chillies and shallots and stir-fry until fragrant. Add the kroeung and continue to stir-fry until it begins to colour. Add the turmeric, fenugreek and sugar.

3 Stir in the chunks of pork loin and stir-fry until golden brown all over. Add the fish sauce and stir well. Pour in the coconut milk and gently stir, and then bring to the boil. Add the butternut squash chunks and the kaffir lime leaves, and reduce the heat to a simmer.

4 Cook uncovered, over medium heat for about 15–20 minutes, until the squash and pork are tender and the sauce has reduced. Season to taste. Garnish the curry with the coriander and mint, and serve with cooked rice or noodles and salad if you like.

Nutritional information per portion: Energy 188Kcal/789kJ; Protein 18g; Carbohydrate 13.2g, of which sugars 12.2g; Fat 7g, of which saturates 2g; Cholesterol 47mg; Calcium 97mg; Fibre 1.7g; Sodium 220mg.

Pork and rice casserole with chilli

This hearty chilli-marinated pork dish with vegetables and rice is very popular in Brazil.
Increase the number of chillies you use if you want to make your taste buds tingle.

SERVES 4–6

500g/1¹/₄lb lean pork, such as fillet
   (tenderloin), cut into strips
60ml/4 tbsp corn oil
1 onion, chopped
1 garlic clove, crushed
1 green (bell) pepper, diced
about 300ml/¹/₂ pint/1¹/₄ cups
   chicken stock
225g/8oz/1 cup long grain rice
150ml/¹/₄ pint/²/₃ cup double
   (heavy) cream
40g/1¹/₂oz/¹/₂ cup freshly grated
   Parmesan cheese
salt and ground black pepper

FOR THE MARINADE

120ml/4fl oz/¹/₂ cup dry white wine
30ml/2 tbsp lemon juice
1 onion, chopped
4 juniper berries, lightly crushed
3 cloves
1 red chilli, seeded and sliced

1 Mix all the marinade ingredients, add the pork and set aside to marinate for 3–4 hours. Transfer the pork to a plate. Strain the marinade and set aside. Heat the oil in a pan and brown the pork. Transfer to a plate.

2 Add the chopped onion, garlic and pepper to the pan and fry for about 6–8 minutes, then return the pork to the pan. Pour in the reserved marinade and the stock. Bring to the boil and season with salt and black pepper, then lower the heat, cover and simmer for 10 minutes until the meat is tender.

3 Preheat the oven to 160°C/325°F/Gas 3. Cook the rice in salted boiling water for 8 minutes. Drain.

4 Spread half the rice over the bottom of a buttered baking dish. Make a layer of meat and vegetables on top, then the rice on top. Stir the cream and 30ml/2 tbsp of the Parmesan into the liquid in which the pork was cooked. Pour over the rice and sprinkle with the remaining Parmesan cheese.

5 Cover the dough with foil and bake for 20 minutes. Remove the foil and cook for 5 minutes more, to brown the top. Serve immediately.

Nutritional information per portion: Energy 490kcal/2040kJ; Protein 31.7g; Carbohydrate 33.3g, of which sugars 3g; Fat 23.9g, of which saturates 10.2g; Cholesterol 91mg; Calcium 342mg; Fibre 0.6g; Sodium 340mg.

Jerk pork with red chillies

This is a Jamaican way of spicing meat or poultry before roasting in the oven or over a fire. Tender pork chops, marinated in aromatic spices, roasted, then served with extra chilli.

SERVES 4

15ml/1 tbsp oil
2 onions, finely chopped
2 fresh red chillies, seeded and
    finely chopped
1 garlic clove, crushed
2.5cm/1in piece fresh root ginger, grated
5ml/1 tsp dried thyme
5ml/1 tsp ground allspice

5ml/1 tsp hot pepper sauce
30ml/2 tbsp rum
grated rind and juice of 1 lime
4 pork chops
salt and ground black pepper
fresh thyme, small red chillies and lime
    wedges, to garnish

1 Heat the oil in a large frying pan. Add the chopped onions and cook for 10 minutes until the onions are soft and translucent.

2 Add the chillies, garlic, ginger, thyme and allspice and fry for 2 minutes. Stir in the hot pepper sauce, rum, lime rind and juice.

3 Lower the heat and simmer gently until the mixture has formed a dark paste. Season with salt and pepper to taste, and set aside to cool.

4 Rub the paste all over the chops, ensuring they are well covered. Place them in a shallow dish, cover and marinate overnight in the refrigerator.

5 Preheat the oven to 190°C/375°F/Gas 5. Place the marinated pork chops on a rack in a roasting pan and roast in the preheated oven for 30 minutes until the pork is fully cooked.

6 Garnish with the chopped thyme, chillies and lime wedges. Serve hot.

Nutritional information per portion: Energy 271kcal/1134kJ; Protein 33.9g; Carbohydrate 9.2g, of which sugars 5.6g; Fat 9.4g, of which saturates 2.5g; Cholesterol 95mg; Calcium 42mg; Fibre 1.4g; Sodium 109mg.

Spicy tandoori chicken

This classic Indian dish has a very unique flavour and is popular all over the world. The mixture of chilli doesn't dominate the other spices, but is nonetheless an essential ingredient.

SERVES 4

8 chicken pieces, such as thighs, drumsticks or halved breast portions, skinned
60ml/4 tbsp lemon juice
10ml/2 tsp salt
175ml/6fl oz/³/4 cup natural (plain) yogurt
5ml/1 tsp chilli powder
5ml/1 tsp garam masala
5ml/1 tsp ground cumin
5ml/1 tsp ground coriander
2 garlic cloves, roughly chopped
2.5cm/1in piece fresh root ginger, roughly chopped
2 fresh green chillies, roughly chopped
red food colouring (optional)
25g/1oz/2 tbsp butter, melted
lemon wedges, to serve

1 Cut deep slashes in the chicken pieces. Mix together the lemon juice and half the salt and rub over the chicken. Set aside for 10 minutes.

2 Mix the natural yogurt, the remaining salt, chilli powder, garam masala, ground cumin and ground coriander in a bowl. Put the garlic, ginger and chillies into a food processor or blender and process until smooth. Scrape out of the processor bowl and stir the mixture into the spiced yogurt.

3 Brush the chicken pieces with food colouring, if using, and put them into a dish that is large enough to hold them in a single layer. Spoon over the marinade, turn the pieces until evenly coated, then cover and chill overnight.

4 Preheat the oven to 220°C/ 425°F/ Gas 7. Put the chicken in a roasting pan and bake for 40 minutes, basting with the melted butter. Serve on a bed of salad, with lemon wedges for squeezing.

Nutritional information per portion: Energy 592kcal/2479kJ; Protein 44g; Carbohydrate 77.5g, of which sugars 4.5g; Fat 11.4g, of which saturates 1.1g; Cholesterol 105mg; Calcium 54mg; Fibre 0.4g; Sodium 826mg.

Sweet and spicy chicken

This chicken dish has a fiery kick, which is mellowed by the combined sweetness of the pineapple juice and maple syrup. The dried chillies, chilli oil and chilli paste provide the heat.

SERVES 3

675g/1¹/₂lb chicken breast fillets
175g/6oz/1¹/₂ cups cornflour (cornstarch)
vegetable oil, for deep-frying
2 green chillies, sliced
2 dried red chillies, seeded and sliced
salt and ground black pepper

FOR THE MARINADE
15ml/1 tbsp white wine
15ml/1 tbsp dark soy sauce
3 garlic cloves, crushed
¹/₄ onion, finely chopped

FOR THE SAUCE
15ml/1 tbsp chilli oil
2.5ml/¹/₂ tsp gochujang chilli paste
30ml/2 tbsp dark soy sauce
7.5ml/1¹/₂ tsp pineapple juice
15 garlic cloves, peeled
30ml/2 tbsp maple syrup
15ml/1 tbsp sugar

1 Slice the chicken into bitesize strips and season with the salt and pepper. Combine all the marinade ingredients in a large bowl. Mix well and add the chicken, rubbing the mixture thoroughly into the meat. Leave to marinate for 20 minutes.

2 Sprinkle the marinated chicken with cornflour, making sure you cover the meat evenly. Fill a wok or medium heavy pan one-third full of oil and heat over high heat to 170°C/340°F, or when a piece of bread dropped in the oil browns in 15 seconds. Add the chicken and deep-fry for 3–5 minutes, or until golden brown.

3 Remove the fried chicken and place on a plate lined with kitchen paper to drain and remove any excess oil from the chicken. Put all the sauce ingredients in a large pan and mix together well, adding all the garlic cloves whole, and heat over medium heat.

4 Once the sauce starts to bubble, add the cooked chicken and stir so that all the meat is coated well with the sauce. Leave to simmer until the sauce has formed a sticky glaze over the chicken, and then add the green and dried chillies. Stir well and transfer to a shallow serving dish and serve hot.

Nutritional information per portion: Energy 655kcal/2749kJ; Protein 56.4g; Carbohydrate 45.3g, of which sugars 14.4g; Fat 28.8g, of which saturates 3.5g; Cholesterol 158mg; Calcium 34mg; Fibre 0.4g; Sodium 1249mg.

Spicy chicken satay

There are few dishes as delicious as satay. This spicy marinade quickly gives an exotic flavour to tender chicken pieces. The satay skewers can be cooked on a barbecue or under the grill.

SERVES 4

30ml/2 tbsp dark soy sauce
juice of ¹/₂ a lemon or 1 lime
2 hot chilli peppers, crushed,
    or 5ml/1 tsp chilli powder
2 shallots, sliced very thin

1 clove of garlic, crushed
    (optional)
15ml/1 tbsp hot water
4 skinless chicken breast fillets,
    about 175g/6oz each

1 Make the marinade. Put the dark soy sauce, lemon juice, chilli peppers, shallots, garlic, if using, and hot water in a large bowl and mix together well. Leave to stand for 30 minutes to let the flavours mingle.

2 Cut the chicken breast fillets into 2.5cm/1in cubes and place in a bowl with the marinade. Mix thoroughly so the chicken is well coated. Cover and leave in a cool place to marinate for at least 1 hour.

3 Soak eight bamboo skewers in cold water for at least 30 minutes so they don't burn while cooking the chicken.

4 Pour the chicken and the marinade into a sieve (strainer) placed over a pan and leave to drain for a few minutes. Set the sieve aside.

5 Add 30ml/2 tbsp hot water to the drained marinade and bring to the boil. Lower the heat and simmer for 2 minutes, then pour into a bowl and leave the marinade to cool.

6 Drain the skewers, thread them with the chicken and cook under a grill (broiler) or on a barbecue for about 10 minutes, turning regularly until the chicken is golden brown and cooked through.

7 Serve the skewers with the cooled marinade as a dip.

Nutritional information per portion: Energy 265kcal/1120kJ; Protein 55.2g; Carbohydrate 3.5g, of which sugars 2g; Fat 3.4g, of which saturates 1g; Cholesterol 158mg; Calcium 19mg; Fibre 0.6g; Sodium 1204mg.

Chicken with basil and chilli

This quick and easy chicken dish is an excellent introduction to cooking with chillies. Thai basil, sometimes known as holy basil, has a pungent flavour that is spicy and sharp.

SERVES 4–6

45ml/3 tbsp vegetable oil

4 garlic cloves, thinly sliced

2–4 fresh red chillies, seeded and finely chopped

450g/1lb skinless boneless chicken breast fillets, cut into bitesize pieces

45ml/3 tbsp Thai fish sauce

10ml/2 tsp dark soy sauce

5ml/1 tsp sugar

10–12 fresh Thai basil leaves

2 fresh red chillies, seeded and finely chopped, and about 20 deep-fried Thai basil leaves, to garnish

1 Heat the oil in a wok or large frying pan. Add the garlic and chillies and stir-fry for 1–2 minutes until the garlic is golden. Take care not to let the garlic burn, otherwise it will taste bitter.

2 Add the pieces of chicken to the wok or pan, in batches if necessary, and stir-fry until the chicken changes colour.

3 Stir in the fish sauce, soy sauce and sugar. Stir-fry the mixture for 3–4 minutes, or until the chicken is cooked through and golden brown in colour.

4 Stir in the fresh Thai basil leaves. Spoon the mixture on to a warm platter. Garnish with the chopped chillies and deep-fried Thai basil leaves and serve immediately.

Nutritional information per portion: Energy 214kcal/899kJ; Protein 28g; Carbohydrate 4g, of which sugars 10g; Fat 10g, of which saturates 1g; Cholesterol 79mg; Calcium 14mg; Fibre 0.1g; Sodium 700mg.

Thai-style chicken with chillies

*This is good home cooking – simple spicy food that you can enjoy as an everyday meal.
The essential elements are the lemon grass and the chillies, so add as much as you dare.*

SERVES 4

15ml/1 tbsp sugar
**30ml/2 tbsp sesame or groundnut
  (peanut) oil**
2 garlic cloves, finely chopped
**2–3 green or red Thai chillies, seeded and
  finely chopped**
2 lemon grass stalks, finely sliced
1 onion, finely sliced
**350g/12oz skinless chicken breast fillets,
  cut into bitesize strips**
30ml/2 tbsp soy sauce
15ml/1 tbsp Thai fish sauce
**1 bunch fresh coriander (cilantro), stalks
  removed, leaves chopped**
salt and ground black pepper
nuoc cham, to serve

1 To make a caramel sauce, put the sugar into a small pan with a few splashes of water, but not enough to soak it.

2 Heat the mixture gently until the sugar has dissolved and turned golden. Set aside.

3 Heat a wok or heavy pan and add the oil. Stir in the garlic, chillies and lemon grass, and cook until they become fragrant.

4 Add the onion and stir-fry for 1 minute, then add the chicken.

5 When the chicken begins to brown, add the soy sauce, fish sauce and caramel sauce. Keep the chicken moving around the wok for a minute or two, then season with a little salt and pepper.

6 Toss the fresh coriander into the chicken and serve immediately with nuoc cham to drizzle over it.

Nutritional information per portion: Energy 202kcal/847kJ; Protein 22g; Carbohydrate 9g, of which sugars 7g; Fat 9g, of which saturates 1g; Cholesterol 61mg; Calcium 32mg; Fibre 0.6g; Sodium 800mg.

Shredded chicken in a chilli sauce

This colourful dish looks very pretty, but has a very spicy sauce. The essential ingredient is the red chillies which provide the heat. Serve with boiled rice and lettuce leaves.

SERVES 6

1 small chicken weighing about
   1.2kg/2^1/$_2$lb, jointed
1 large carrot, peeled
1 celery heart
1 thin leek
2 litres/3^1/$_2$ pints/8 cups water
salt

FOR THE CHILLI SAUCE

3 red chillies, seeded and
   roughly chopped
6 medium slices white bread,
   reduced to crumbs
175ml/6fl oz/^{3}/$_4$ cup evaporated milk

90ml/6 tbsp vegetable oil
1 medium onion, finely chopped
50g/2oz/^{1}/$_2$ cup ground almonds
50g/2oz/^{2}/$_3$ cup grated Parmesan cheese

TO SERVE

6 portions white rice mixed with corn
6 lettuce leaves
500g/1^1/$_4$lb King Edward potatoes, boiled
   in their skins, then peeled and sliced
6 kalamata olives, pitted
3 hard-boiled eggs, halved
chilli strips, to garnish (optional)

1 Place the chicken in a pan of salted water with the carrot, celery and leek. Bring to the boil and skim, then simmer covered, for 40 minutes. Lift out the chicken and strain and reserve the stock. Shred the chicken flesh. Set aside.

2 Put the chillies in a blender or food processor with 100ml/3^1/$_2$fl oz/scant ^{1}/$_2$ cup water and purée. Set aside. Soak the breadcrumbs in the evaporated milk for 5 minutes, blend to a smooth paste and set aside.

3 Heat the oil in a pan and fry the onion for 10 minutes, until it browns. Add the chilli purée and cook for 3 minutes. Add the breadcrumb mixture. Stir in the shredded chicken and add 750ml/ 1^1/$_4$ pints/3 cups of the reserved stock. Continue to cook, stirring, until the sauce is creamy and smooth. Add the ground almonds and the Parmesan cheese and simmer for 5 more minutes.

4 Arrange a portion of rice with corn on each plate. Place a lettuce leaf beside the rice. Place three slices of potato on top of each lettuce leaf. Spoon some of the chicken mixture on top and garnish with an olive and half a hard-boiled egg. Add a few strips of chilli, if you like.

Nutritional information per portion: Energy 495kcal/2062kJ; Protein 34.7g; Carbohydrate 20.9g, of which sugars 6.9g; Fat 30.8g, of which saturates 9.1g; Cholesterol 141mg; Calcium 249mg; Fibre 1.6g; Sodium 368mg.

Chilli chicken and okra stew

The combination of okra pieces and tender chicken coated in a rich, spicy tomato and chilli sauce makes an ideal family meal. It is totally fuss-free, taking very little time and effort to prepare.

SERVES 4

15ml/1 tbsp olive oil

4 chicken thighs

1 large onion, finely chopped

2 garlic cloves, finely crushed

2 fresh red chillies, seeded and
   finely chopped

120ml/4fl oz/$\frac{1}{2}$ cup water

350g/12oz okra

2 large tomatoes, finely chopped

salt

boiled white rice or polenta, to serve

hot chilli oil (optional)

1 Heat the oil in a wide pan over low heat. Season the chicken thighs with salt and add them to the pan, skin side down. Cook until golden brown, turn them over and add the chopped onion.

2 Sauté for 5 minutes, until the onion has softened; then add the garlic and chopped chillies. Cook for a further 2 minutes. Add half the water to the pan and bring to the boil. Lower the heat, cover and cook for 30 minutes.

3 Trim the okra and slice into thin rounds. Add to the pan with the tomatoes. Season with salt and pour in the remaining water. Cover and simmer gently for about 10–15 minutes, or until the chicken pieces are tender and fully cooked. The chicken is ready when the flesh can be pulled off the bone easily. Serve immediately with boiled white rice or polenta, and offer some hot chilli oil on the side, if you like.

Nutritional information per portion: Energy 235kcal/988kJ; Protein 28.6g; Carbohydrate 13.2g, of which sugars 11.9g; Fat 8g, of which saturates 1.2g; Cholesterol 72mg; Calcium 76mg; Fibre 2.4g; Sodium 204mg.

Fiery chicken casserole

This warming stew is filled with flavoursome vegetables and spices. Red and green chillies and a spicy gochujang chilli paste supply a vivid red colour and give the chicken a zingy quality.

SERVES 4

3 potatoes
1 carrot
2 onions
1 chicken, about 800g/1³/₄lb
30ml/2 tbsp mirin or rice wine
salt and ground black pepper
30ml/2 tbsp vegetable oil
2 garlic cloves, crushed
3 green chillies, seeded and sliced
1 red chilli, seeded and sliced
15ml/1 tbsp sesame oil
salt and ground black pepper
1 spring onion (scallion), finely sliced,
   to garnish

FOR THE SEASONING

15ml/1 tbsp sesame seeds
10ml/2 tsp light soy sauce
30ml/2 tbsp gochujang chilli paste
45ml/3 tbsp Korean chilli powder

1 Peel the potatoes and cut into bitesize pieces. Soak in cold water for 15–20 minutes and drain. Peel the carrot and onions and cut into pieces. Cut the chicken, with skin and bone, into bitesize pieces and mix with the mirin or rice wine and salt and pepper. Stir to coat and leave for 10 minutes.

2 Heat 15ml/1 tbsp vegetable oil in a frying pan or wok, and quickly stir-fry the crushed garlic. Add the chicken and stir-fry, draining off any fat. When lightly browned, place the chicken on kitchen paper to remove any excess oil.

3 For the seasoning, grind the sesame seeds in a mortar and pestle. Combine with the soy sauce, gochujang paste and chilli powder in a bowl.

4 Heat the remaining oil. Add the potatoes, carrot and onions. Cook gently. Add the chicken. Pour in water to cover. Bring to the boil then add the chilli seasoning. Simmer until the sauce has reduced by a third. Add the chillies and simmer until the liquid has thickened slightly. Add the sesame oil, before transferring to deep serving bowls and garnish with the spring onion.

Nutritional information per portion: Energy 470kcal/1955kJ; Protein 27.4g; Carbohydrate 20.4g, of which sugars 4.7g; Fat 31.5g, of which saturates 7.5g; Cholesterol 128mg; Calcium 56mg; Fibre 2.3g; Sodium 296mg.

Spicy green chicken curry

The chilli spice mixture forms the basis of this dish, providing a warming heat, while the coconut milk creates a rich sauce that is sweet with fruit and fragrant with herbs and aromatic spices.

SERVES 4

1/2 **bunch fresh coriander (cilantro)**
4 **garlic cloves, chopped**
15ml/1 **tbsp chopped fresh root ginger**
2–3 **chillies, chopped**
1 **onion, chopped**
juice of 1 lemon
pinch of cayenne pepper
2.5ml/1/2 **tsp curry powder**
2.5ml/1/2 **tsp ground cumin**
2–3 **pinches of ground cloves**
large pinch of ground coriander
3 **skinless chicken breast fillets or thighs**
30ml/2 **tbsp vegetable oil**
2 **cinnamon sticks**
250ml/8fl oz/1 **cup chicken stock**
250ml/8fl oz/1 **cup coconut milk**
15–30ml/1–2 **tbsp sugar**
1–2 **bananas**
1/4 **pineapple, peeled and chopped**
handful of sultanas (golden raisins)
handful of raisins or currants
2–3 **sprigs of mint, thinly sliced**
juice of 1 lemon

1 Roughly chop the coriander, and put into a processor or blender with the garlic, ginger, chillies, onion, lemon juice, cayenne pepper, curry powder, cumin, cloves, ground coriander and season with salt. Process to a smooth paste.

2 Cut the chicken portions into bitesize pieces. Toss together the chicken pieces with about 15–30ml/1–2 tbsp of the spice mixture and set aside.

3 Heat the oil in a wok or frying pan, then add the remaining spice mixture and cook over a medium heat, stirring, for 10 minutes, or until the paste is lightly browned.

4 To make the curry sauce, stir in the cinnamon sticks, chicken stock, coconut milk and sugar into the browned spice mixture, bring to the boil, and then reduce the heat and simmer for a further 10 minutes more.

5 Stir the chicken pieces into the sauce and cook them for 2 minutes, or until the chicken becomes opaque in colour.

6 Meanwhile, thickly slice the bananas. Stir all the fruit into the pan and cook for 1–2 minutes. Add the mint and lemon juice. Serve immediately, with flat bread and fresh lemons if you like.

Nutritional information per portion: Energy 383kcal/1622kJ; Protein 29.5g; Carbohydrate 11.9g, of which sugars 11.7g; Fat 10.4g, of which saturates 2g; Cholesterol 140mg; Calcium 78mg; Fibre 1.1g; Sodium 462mg.

Chilli-marinated chicken with coconut milk

You need to marinate the chicken legs overnight in an aromatic blend of yogurt and spices before gently simmering with hot green chillies in creamy coconut milk. Serve with rice or Indian breads.

SERVES 4

1.6kg/3½lb large chicken drumsticks
30ml/2 tbsp sunflower oil
400ml/14fl oz/1⅔ cups coconut milk
4–6 large green chillies, halved
45ml/3 tbsp finely chopped
   coriander (cilantro)
salt and ground black pepper
natural (plain) yogurt, to drizzle

FOR THE MARINADE

15ml/1 tbsp crushed cardamom seeds
15ml/1 tbsp grated fresh root ginger
10ml/2 tsp finely grated garlic
105ml/7 tbsp natural (plain) yogurt
2 green chillies, seeded and chopped
5ml/1 tsp ground cumin
5ml/1 tsp ground coriander
5ml/1 tsp turmeric
finely grated rind and juice of 1 lime

1 Make the marinade. Place the cardamom, ginger, garlic, half the yogurt, green chillies, cumin, coriander, turmeric and lime zest and juice into a processor or blender. Process the mixture until smooth, season and pour into a large glass bowl.

2 Add the chicken drumsticks to the marinade and toss to coat evenly. Cover the bowl and marinate in the refrigerator overnight. Heat the oil in a large, non-stick wok over low heat.

3 Remove the chicken from the marinade, reserving the marinade. Add the chicken to the wok and brown all over, then add the coconut milk, remaining yogurt, reserved marinade and green chillies and bring to a boil.

4 Reduce the heat and simmer uncovered for 30–35 minutes. Check the seasoning, adding more if needed. Stir in the coriander, ladle into warmed bowls and serve immediately. Drizzle with yogurt if you like.

Nutritional information per portion: Energy 706kcal/2935kJ; Protein 48.1g; Carbohydrate 15.8g, of which sugars 15.6g; Fat 50.4g, of which saturates 12.8g; Cholesterol 240mg; Calcium 91mg; Fibre 1.5g; Sodium 305mg.

Spicy chicken couscous

This is an easy recipe to make and is perfect for entertaining. A few key ingredients flavour the couscous – the chicken and carrot adding texture and colour, while the chillies provide the fire.

SERVES 6

1 small organic chicken

2 onions, quartered

2 cinnamon sticks

4 cardamom pods

4 cloves

2 bay leaves

450g/1lb/2¹/₂ cups couscous, rinsed
   and drained

30ml/2 tbsp ghee, or 30ml/2 tbsp olive
   oil with a knob of butter

1 onion, finely chopped

2–3 cloves garlic, finely chopped

1 red or green chilli, seeded and very
   finely chopped

1 medium carrot, finely diced

5–10ml/1–2 tsp ground cinnamon

small bunch of fresh coriander (cilantro),
   finely chopped

sea salt and ground black pepper

1 Place the whole chicken in a deep pan with the onions, cinnamon sticks, cardamom pods, cloves and bay leaves and cover with water. Bring the water to the boil, reduce the heat and simmer for 1 hour, or until the chicken is tender.

2 Transfer the cooked chicken to a plate. Strain the stock into a large bowl, then return the strained stock to the pan and boil it over high heat for about 30 minutes, until it reduces.

3 Remove and discard the skin from the chicken and tear the flesh into thin strips, or cut it into bitesize chunks. Cover the chicken and keep warm.

4 Transfer the couscous into a bowl and pour in about 500ml/17fl oz/2 cups warm water. Add 5ml/1 tsp salt, stir the couscous once, then place a clean dish towel over the bowl and leave for 10 minutes for the couscous to swell.

5 Meanwhile, heat the ghee or olive oil and butter in a heavy, shallow pan and stir in the onions and garlic. Cook for a minute to soften, then add the chilli and carrot and sauté for 2–3 minutes, until they begin to colour.

6 Stir the cinnamon and half the coriander into the onion mixture, then add the couscous, forking through it constantly to mix well and make sure the grains don't clump together, until it is heated through.

7 Turn the couscous into a warmed serving dish and arrange the shredded chicken on top. Season the reduced stock with salt and pepper and spoon some of it over the chicken to moisten.

8 Sprinkle the remaining chopped coriander on top to garnish, and pour the rest of the stock into a large serving bowl for spooning over the individual portions.

Nutritional information per portion: Energy 376kcal/1574kJ; Protein 31.9g; Carbohydrate 44.6g, of which sugars 4g; Fat 8.8g, of which saturates 3.5g; Cholesterol 70mg; Calcium 49mg; Fibre 1.1g; Sodium 128mg

Spicy turkey and corn stew

This fiery stew is very simple to make. The turkey goes particularly well with the corn paste and the hot chilli sauce is gloriously fiery. Serve with plain boiled rice for a tasty and filling meal.

SERVES 4

6 corn cobs
90ml/6 tbsp vegetable oil
500g/1¹/₄lb skinless turkey breast fillet, cut into 2cm/³/₄in cubes
1 medium onion, finely chopped
2 garlic cloves, sliced or crushed
2 red chillies, seeded, blended to a purée in 60ml/4 tbsp water
500ml/17fl oz/generous 2 cups chicken stock
salt
chopped parsley, to garnish
boiled rice, to serve (optional)

1 Using a sharp knife, strip the kernels from the corn on the cob. Put them in batches in a blender or food processor and blend to a paste.

2 Heat the oil in a large pan and fry the turkey over a high heat for 8–10 minutes, until golden on all sides. Stir in the onion and garlic, reduce the heat slightly and cook until the onion is caramelized.

3 Add the chilli purée to the mixture and cook for a further 3 minutes, then pour in the chicken stock. Bring to the boil, then reduce the heat and simmer for 20 minutes. Season to taste with salt.

4 Add the puréed corn and simmer for a further 15 minutes, until thick. Garnish with parsley and serve the turkey stew with boiled rice.

Nutritional information per portion: Energy 472kcal/1980kJ; Protein 34g; Carbohydrate 42g, of which sugars 15.9g; Fat 19.8g, of which saturates 2.4g; Cholesterol 61mg; Calcium 24mg; Fibre 2.5g; Sodium 461mg.

Chilli-spiced poussin

When you are short of time, these sizzling poussins make a quick and spicy alternative to the traditional roast dinner. The chilli powder adds depth and richness to the meat.

SERVES 4

2 poussins, 675g/1¹/₂lb each
15ml/1 tbsp chilli powder
15ml/1 tbsp ground cumin
45ml/3 tbsp olive oil
salt and ground black pepper
salad leaves, to serve

1 Spatchcock one poussin: remove the wishbone and split the bird along each side of the backbone and remove it. Press down on the breastbone to flatten the bird.

2 Push a metal skewer through the wings and breast to keep the bird flat, then push a second skewer through the thighs and breast. Spatchcock the second poussin in the same way.

3 Combine the chilli, cumin, oil and seasoning. Brush over the poussins. Preheat the grill (broiler). Lay the birds, skin side down, on a grill rack and grill (broil) for 15 minutes. Turn over and grill for a further 15 minutes until cooked through.

4 Remove the skewers and split each bird in half along the breastbone. Drizzle over the juices, and serve with fresh salad leaves.

Nutritional information per portion: Energy 465kcal/1936kJ; Protein 36.6g; Carbohydrate 1.3g, of which sugars 0g; Fat 35.1g, of which saturates 8.4g; Cholesterol 189mg; Calcium 20mg; Fibre 0g; Sodium 131mg.

Duck sausages with chilli plum sauce

These rich duck sausages are best when baked in their own juices. Creamy mashed sweet potatoes and the spicy plum sauce wonderfully complement and contrast the richness of the meat.

SERVES 4

8–12 duck sausages

FOR THE SWEET POTATO MASH
1.5kg/3¼lb sweet potatoes, cut
   into chunks
25g/1oz/2 tbsp butter
60ml/4 tbsp milk
salt and ground black pepper

FOR THE PLUM SAUCE
30ml/2 tbsp olive oil
1 small onion, chopped
1 small red chilli, seeded and
   finely chopped
450g/1lb plums, stoned (pitted)
   and chopped
30ml/2 tbsp red wine vinegar
45ml/3 tbsp clear honey

1 Preheat the oven to 190°C/375°F/Gas 5. Arrange the duck sausages in a single layer in a large, shallow ovenproof dish and bake, uncovered, for 25–30 minutes, turning the sausages two or three times during cooking, to ensure that they brown and cook evenly.

2 Meanwhile, put the sweet potatoes in a pan and pour in enough water to cover them. Bring to the boil, reduce the heat and simmer for 20 minutes, or until tender.

3 Drain and mash the sweet potatoes, then place the pan over low heat. Stir frequently for about 5 minutes to dry out the mashed potatoes. Beat in the butter and milk, and season with salt and pepper.

4 Heat the oil in a frying pan and fry the onion and chilli gently for about 5 minutes until the onion is soft and translucent. Stir in the plums, vinegar and honey, then simmer gently for about 10 minutes.

5 Divide the cooked sausages among four individual plates or bowls and serve immediately with the sweet potato mash and piquant plum sauce.

Nutritional information per portion: Energy 894kcal/3755kJ; Protein 17.8g; Carbohydrate 110.8g, of which sugars 42.9g; Fat 45.5g, of which saturates 17.9g; Cholesterol 67mg; Calcium 170mg; Fibre 11.6g; Sodium 1052mg.

Duck with spicy orange sauce

This Asian-style dish of duck with orange is inspired by the French classic caneton à l'orange, but the use of the spices and chillies makes this zesty version taste delightfully different.

SERVES 3

4 duck legs

4 garlic cloves, crushed

50g/2oz fresh root ginger, peeled and finely sliced

2 lemon grass stalks, trimmed, cut into 3 pieces and crushed

2 dried whole red Thai chillies

15ml/1 tbsp palm sugar (jaggery)

5ml/1 tsp Chinese five-spice powder

30ml/2 tbsp nuoc cham or tuk trey

900ml/1¹⁄₂ pints/3³⁄₄ cups fresh orange juice

sea salt and ground black pepper

watercress and orange rind, to serve

1 Place the duck legs, skin side down, in a wok or a large heavy pan with a lid. Cook the legs on both sides over medium heat for about 10 minutes, until browned and crispy. Transfer them to a plate and set aside.

2 Stir the garlic, ginger, lemon grass and chillies into the fat left in the pan, and cook until golden. Add the palm sugar, five-spice powder and nuoc cham or tuk trey Stir in the orange juice and place the duck legs back in the pan.

3 Cover the pan and gently cook the duck for 1–2 hours, until the meat is tender and the sauce has reduced. Season with salt and pepper, and serve with watercress and thin slices of orange rind.

Nutritional information per portion: Energy 280Kcal/1181kJ; Protein 31g; Carbohydrate 23.8g, of which sugars 23.8g; Fat 10g, of which saturates 2g; Cholesterol 165mg; Calcium 48mg; Fibre 0.4g; Sodium 250mg.

Smoked duck in a chilli paste

This dish features tender duck, smeared with lots of fresh chillies, spices and herbs and slowly roasted until the aromatic meat is so tender it falls off the bone.

SERVES 4

1.8kg/4lb oven-ready duck
1 large banana leaf or foil
salt and ground black pepper

FOR THE SPICE PASTE

6–8 shallots, chopped
4 garlic cloves, chopped
4 chillies, seeded and chopped
25g/1oz fresh root ginger, chopped
50g/2oz fresh turmeric, chopped, or
   25ml/1$^{1}/_{2}$ tbsp ground turmeric
2 lemon grass stalks, chopped
4 lime leaves, crumbled
4 candlenuts, chopped
10ml/2 tsp coriander seeds
15ml/1 tbsp shrimp paste
15–30ml/1–2 tbsp water

1 First make the paste. Using a mortar and pestle or a food processor, grind all the ingredients, except the shrimp paste and water, together to form a smooth mixture, then add the shrimp paste and water and mix together.

2 Preheat the oven to 160°C/325°F/Gas 3. Rub the spice paste all over the duck, inside and out, and sprinkle the duck with salt and pepper.

3 Place the duck in the centre of the banana leaf or a sheet of foil. If using a banana leaf, secure it with string to hold in place. If using foil, tuck in the short sides and fold the long sides over the top to form a parcel, then place in a roasting pan.

4 Roast the duck for 4–5 hours, then open the parcel to reveal the top of the duck and roast for a further 30–45 minutes to brown the skin. Serve.

Nutritional information per portion: Energy 234kcal/982kJ; Protein 26.9g; Carbohydrate 12.8g, of which sugars 8.4g; Fat 8.8g, of which saturates 2.7g; Cholesterol 135mg; Calcium 75mg; Fibre 3g; Sodium 161mg.

Chargrilled quails in a chilli marinade

This is a simple and tasty way of serving small birds, such as quails, poussins or grouse. The sharp, spicy marinade tenderizes the meat, as well as giving it a zesty flavour. Served straight off the grill with warm flat bread and a crunchy salad, they are delicious for lunch or supper.

SERVES 4

4 quails, cleaned and boned
juice of 4 pomegranates
juice of 1 lemon
30ml/2 tbsp olive oil
1 red pepper, chopped, or 5ml/1 tsp
   chilli powder

30–45ml/2–3 tbsp thick and creamy
   natural (plain) yogurt
salt
1 bunch of fresh flat leaf parsley
seeds of 1/2 pomegranate,
   to garnish

1 Soak eight wooden skewers in hot water for about 15 minutes, then drain. Thread one skewer through the wings of each bird and a second skewer through the legs to keep them together.

2 Place the skewered birds in a wide, shallow dish. Beat the pomegranate juice and lemon juice with the oil and the red pepper or chilli powder. Pour the mixture over the quails and rub it into the skin until the birds are covered in the marinade.

3 Cover with foil and leave to marinate in a cold place or the refrigerator for 2–3 hours, turning the birds over occasionally.

4 Get the barbecue or griddle pan ready for cooking. Lift the birds out of the marinade and pour the remaining marinade into a small bowl. Beat the yogurt into the leftover marinade and season with a little salt.

5 Brush some of the yogurt mixture over the skewered birds and place them on the prepared barbecue. Cook for 4–5 minutes on each side, brushing with the yogurt as they cook to form a crust.

6 Chop some of the parsley and lay the rest on a serving dish. Place the cooked quails on the parsley and garnish with the pomegranate seeds and the chopped parsley. Serve hot.

Nutritional information per portion: Energy 288kcal/1207kJ; Protein 37.4g; Carbohydrate 5.8g, of which sugars 5.8g; Fat 13g, of which saturates 2.7g; Cholesterol 0mg; Calcium 84mg; Fibre 0.5g; Sodium 111mg.

Vegetarian dishes and accompaniments

Chillies are great for highlighting other flavours, and nowhere is this more apparent than when they are added to vegetable and vegetarian dishes, such as gratins and curries. Chillies also taste great in salads too, from a simple mixture of broad bean, potato and cheese to a colourful combination of fresh fruit and raw vegetables.

Chilli cheese tortilla

If you love red-hot scorching flavours, then this tasty tortilla will not disappoint. It is spiked with plenty of fresh jalapeño chillies, and the spicy chilli salsa provides extra heat.

SERVES 4

45ml/3 tbsp sunflower or olive oil
1 small onion, thinly sliced
2–3 fresh green jalapeño chillies, seeded and sliced
200g/7oz cold cooked potato, thinly sliced
150g/5oz/1¼ cups grated cheese
6 eggs, beaten
salt and ground black pepper
fresh herbs and chilli, to garnish

FOR THE SALSA

500g/1¼lb fresh, flavoursome tomatoes, peeled, seeded and finely chopped
1 fresh mild green chilli, seeded and finely chopped
2 garlic cloves, crushed
45ml/3 tbsp chopped fresh coriander (cilantro)
juice of 1 lime
2.5ml/½ tsp salt

1 Make the salsa by putting all the salsa ingredients in a bowl. Mix well, cover and set aside.

2 Heat 15ml/1 tbsp of the oil in a large frying pan and gently fry the onion and jalapeños for 5 minutes, stirring until softened. Add the potato and cook for 5 minutes until lightly browned, keeping the slices whole. Using a slotted spoon, transfer the cooked vegetables to a warm plate.

3 Wipe the pan with kitchen paper, then add the remaining oil and heat until really hot. Return the vegetables to the pan. Sprinkle the cheese over the top and season.

4 Pour in the beaten egg, making sure that it seeps under the vegetables. Cook over low heat, stirring, until set. Serve hot or cold, in wedges, with the salsa. Garnish with fresh herbs and chilli.

Nutritional information per portion: Energy 375kcal/1563kJ; Protein 19.3g; Carbohydrate 13.5g, of which sugars 5.7g; Fat 27.1g, of which saturates 10g; Cholesterol 315mg; Calcium 305mg; Fibre 2.6g; Sodium 589mg.

Spicy vegetable gratin

Subtly spiced with curry powder, turmeric, coriander and chilli powder, this rich and flavoursome gratin is substantial enough to serve on its own for lunch or supper.

SERVES 4

2 large potatoes, about 450g/1lb total weight

2 sweet potatoes, about 275g/10oz total weight

175g/6oz celeriac

15ml/1 tbsp unsalted butter

5ml/1 tsp curry powder

5ml/1 tsp ground turmeric

2.5ml/¹/₂ tsp ground coriander

5ml/1 tsp mild chilli powder

3 shallots, chopped

150ml/¹/₄ pint/²/₃ cup single (light) cream

150ml/¹/₄ pint/²/₃ cup milk

salt and ground black pepper

chopped fresh parsley, to garnish

1 Cut the potatoes, sweet potatoes and celeriac into thin, even slices using a sharp knife and quickly place them in a bowl of cold water to prevent them from discolouring.

2 Preheat the oven to 180°C/350°F/Gas 4. Heat half the butter in a pan, add the curry powder, ground turmeric and coriander and half the chilli powder. Cook for 2 minutes. Drain the vegetables and place them in a bowl, add the spice mixture and shallots and mix well.

3 Arrange the vegetables in a shallow baking dish, and season well. Mix together the cream and milk, pour the mixture over the vegetables, then sprinkle the remaining chilli powder on top.

4 Cover the dish with baking parchment and bake for 45 minutes. Remove the baking parchment, dot the vegetables with the remaining butter and bake for a further 50 minutes, or until the top is golden brown. Serve garnished with parsley.

Nutritional information per portion: Energy 268kcal/1129kJ; Protein 5.8g; Carbohydrate 37.7g, of which sugars 9.8g; Fat 11.6g, of which saturates 7.1g; Cholesterol 31mg; Calcium 127mg; Fibre 3.6g; Sodium 117mg.

Peppers with cheese and chilli filling

Sweet peppers and chillies are natural companions, so it isn't surprising that they work so well together in this traditional Bulgarian dish. Serve with a salad of chopped tomatoes and cucumber.

SERVES 3–4

4 red, yellow or green (bell) peppers
    or long peppers
50g/2oz/^{1}/$_2$ cup plain (all-purpose) flour
1 egg, beaten
olive oil, for shallow-frying
cucumber and tomato salad,
    to serve
salt and pepper

FOR THE FILLING

1 egg
90g/3^1/$_2$oz/generous ^{1}/$_2$ cup finely
    crumbled feta cheese
30ml/2 tbsp chopped fresh parsley
1 small fresh red or green chilli, seeded
    and finely chopped

1 Preheat the grill (broiler). Using a sharp knife, slit open the peppers lengthways on one side only, enabling you to scoop out the seeds and remove the cores while leaving the peppers in one piece.

2 Place the peppers in a grill (broiling) pan. Cook under medium heat until the skin is charred and blackened. Place the peppers in a plastic bag, tie the top to keep the steam in and set aside for 20 minutes.

3 Using a sharp knife, carefully peel away the skin from the peppers.

4 Beat together all the ingredients for the filling in a bowl. Divide and spread the filling evenly among the four peppers.

5 Once the peppers are filled, reshape the peppers to look whole. Season the flour with salt and black pepper. Dip the peppers into the flour, then into the beaten egg and then the flour again.

6 Heat the olive oil for shallow-frying in a large pan and fry the filled peppers over a gentle heat for 6–8 minutes, turning once with a spatula, until they are golden brown and the filling is set. Drain the peppers on kitchen paper before serving with a cucumber and tomato salad.

Nutritional information per portion: Energy 344kcal/1430kJ; Protein 9.9g; Carbohydrate 21.6g, of which sugars 11.5g; Fat 24.8g, of which saturates 6.4g; Cholesterol 111mg; Calcium 152mg; Fibre 3.8g; Sodium 371mg.

Aubergines with lemon grass and chillies

One of the treasures of Malaysia is the round, orange aubergine, which has a delicate flavour. It is particularly tasty cooked in coconut milk with chilli powder, ginger and lemon grass.

SERVES 4

15ml/1 tbsp ground turmeric

5ml/1 tsp chilli powder

3 slender aubergines (eggplants) or
   8 baby aubergines, cut in wedges

45ml/3 tbsp vegetable or groundnut
   (peanut) oil

2 lemon grass stalks, trimmed,
   halved and bruised

600ml/1 pint/2½ cups coconut milk

salt and ground black pepper

cooked rice, to serve

2 green chillies, to garnish

FOR THE SPICE PASTE

4–6 dried red chillies

4 garlic cloves, chopped

4 shallots, chopped

25g/1oz fresh root ginger

2 lemon grass stalks

1 First make the spice paste. Soak the dried red chillies in warm water until soft, then squeeze them dry and remove the seeds. Peel and chop the ginger, and then trim and chop the lemon grass.

2 Using a mortar and pestle or food processor, grind or blend the chillies, garlic, shallots, ginger and lemon grass to a coarse paste.

3 Mix the turmeric and chilli powder together and rub over the aubergine.

4 Heat the oil in a wok or heavy pan. Stir in the paste and lemon grass. Add the aubergine, and cook until lightly browned. Pour in the coconut milk, stir well, and boil until it thickens slightly. Reduce the heat and cook gently for 15–20 minutes or until the aubergine is tender. Season with salt and pepper.

5 Slice the green chillies in half and remove the seeds, then finely chop. Serve with the cooked rice and garnish with sliced chillies.

Nutritional information per portion: Energy 154kcal/644kJ; Protein 6.2g; Carbohydrate 11.9g, of which sugars 11g; Fat 9.5g, of which saturates 1.4g; Cholesterol 38mg; Calcium 175mg; Fibre 3g; Sodium 497mg.

Spicy aubergine curry

Aubergines are the perfect vegetable to use for a spicy vegetable curry, as they are delightfully tender and absorb all the hot and aromatic flavours of the dried chilli.

SERVES 4–6

15ml/1 tbsp vegetable oil
4 garlic cloves, crushed
2 shallots, sliced
2 dried chillies
45ml/3 tbsp kroeung
15ml/1 tbsp palm sugar (jaggery)
600ml/1 pint/2½ cups coconut milk
250ml/8fl oz/1 cup vegetable stock
4 aubergines (eggplants), trimmed and
    cut into bitesize pieces
6 kaffir lime leaves
1 bunch fresh basil, stalks removed
2 limes, cut into quarters
salt and ground black pepper
cooked jasmine rice, to serve

1 Heat the oil in a wok or a large heavy pan with a lid. Stir in the crushed garlic, sliced shallots and whole dried chillies, and stir-fry until they begin to colour. Stir in the kroeung and palm sugar and continue to fry, stirring constantly, until the spice mixture begins to darken.

2 Pour the coconut milk and the vegetable stock into the pan, stirring until thoroughly combined. Add the bitesize aubergine pieces to the pan, and then the lime leaves.

3 Partially cover the pan with the lid, lower the heat and simmer gently for about 25 minutes, stirring occasionally until the aubergines are cooked and tender. Stir in the fresh basil and check the seasoning, adding more if needed.

4 Serve with cooked rice and squeeze the juice from the limes on top.

Nutritional information per portion: Energy 72kcal/305kJ; Protein 1.6g; Carbohydrate 11.2g, of which sugars 10.7g; Fat 3g, of which saturates 1g; Cholesterol 0mg; Calcium 46mg; Fibre 2.8g; Sodium 113mg.

Indian-spiced parsnip curry

The sweet flavour of parsnips goes very well with the chillies and spices in this Indian-style vegetable stew. Serve it with plain yogurt and offer Indian breads to mop up the sauce.

SERVES 4

200g/7oz dried chickpeas, soaked
    overnight in cold water, then drained
7 garlic cloves, finely chopped
1 small onion, chopped
5cm/2in piece fresh root ginger, chopped
2 green chillies, seeded and chopped
75ml/5 tbsp water
450ml/³/₄ pint/scant 2 cups water
60ml/4 tbsp groundnut (peanut) oil
5ml/1 tsp cumin seeds
10ml/2 tsp ground coriander

5ml/1 tsp ground turmeric
2.5–5ml/¹/₂–1 tsp chilli powder
50g/2oz cashew nuts, toasted and ground
250g/9oz tomatoes, peeled and chopped
900g/2lb parsnips, cut in chunks
5ml/1 tsp ground cumin seeds
juice of 1 lime, to taste
salt and ground black pepper
fresh coriander (cilantro) leaves and
    toasted cashew nuts, to garnish
sour cream, to serve (optional)

1 Put the soaked chickpeas in a pan, cover with cold water and bring to the boil. Boil vigorously for 10 minutes, then reduce the heat so that the water boils steadily. Cook for 1–1¹/₂ hours, or until the chickpeas are tender. Drain.

2 Set 10ml/2 tsp of the garlic aside, then place the rest in a food processor or blender with the onion, ginger and half the green chillies. Add 75ml/5 tbsp water, and process until the mixture is smooth.

3 Heat the oil in a large, deep, frying pan and cook the cumin seeds for 30 seconds. Stir in the ground coriander, turmeric, chilli powder and the ground cashew nuts. Add the ginger and chilli paste and cook, stirring frequently. Add the tomatoes and stir-fry until the mixture begins to turn red-brown. Mix in the chickpeas and parsnips with the main batch of water, 5ml/1 tsp salt and plenty of black pepper. Bring to the boil then simmer, uncovered, for 15–20 minutes.

4 Reduce the liquid, if necessary, by boiling fiercely. Add the ground cumin with more salt and lime juice to taste. Stir in the reserved garlic and green chilli. Sprinkle the coriander leaves and toasted cashew nuts over and serve straight away with sour cream, if using.

Nutritional information per portion: Energy 506kcal/2124kJ; Protein 18.4g; Carbohydrate 60.1g, of which sugars 18.2g; Fat 23.1g, of which saturates 3.4g; Cholesterol 0mg; Calcium 192mg; Fibre 17.1g; Sodium 86mg.

Spicy vegetable and chana dhal curry

Chana dhal is a very small type of chickpea grown in India. It has a nutty taste and gives fabulous earthy flavour to the food which combines extremely well with the heat of the chilli.

SERVES 4–6

175g/6oz/²/₃ cup chana dhal or yellow
   split peas, washed
450ml/³/₄ pint/scant 2 cups water
60ml/4 tbsp vegetable oil
2 fresh green chillies, chopped
1 onion, chopped
2 cloves garlic, crushed
5cm/2in piece fresh root ginger, grated
6–8 curry leaves
5ml/1 tsp chilli powder
5ml/1 tsp ground turmeric
450g/1lb marrow (large zucchini),
   courgettes (zucchini), squash or
   pumpkin, peeled, pithed and sliced
60ml/4 tbsp tamarind juice
2 tomatoes, chopped
salt
a handful fresh coriander (cilantro)
   leaves, chopped

1 Fill a large pan with water and pour the chana dhal or yellow split peas into the water. Season the water with salt, and cook for about 30 minutes until the chana dhal grains or split peas are tender but not mushy. Set aside.

2 Heat the oil in a large pan and fry the chillies, onion, garlic, ginger, curry leaves, chilli powder, turmeric and salt until the onions have softened and started to brown.

3 Stir in the marrow, courgettes, squash or pumpkin pieces to the chilli onion mixture and mix together well.

4 Add the cooked chana dhal or split peas and the cooking water and bring to the boil.

5 Add the tamarind juice, tomatoes and coriander, reserving a few for a garnish. Simmer until the vegetable pieces are cooked. Serve hot.

Nutritional information per portion: Energy 198kcal/832kJ; Protein 8.3g; Carbohydrate 24.6g, of which sugars 7.6g; Fat 8.1g, of which saturates 0.9g; Cholesterol 0mg; Calcium 45mg; Fibre 3g; Sodium 18mg.

Mixed bean and tomato chilli

Here, mixed beans, fiery red chilli and freshly chopped coriander are simmered in a herb and tomato sauce to make a spicy vegetarian chilli which is delicious served with crusty bread.

SERVES 4

400g/14oz jar tomato and herb sauce
1 fresh red chilli, seeded and thinly sliced
2 x 400g/14oz cans mixed beans,
    drained and rinsed
large handful of fresh coriander
    (cilantro), chopped
natural (plain) yogurt, to serve
chopped celery, to garnish
red chilli, finely sliced, to garnish

1 Pour the tomato and herb sauce, chilli and mixed beans into a large pan with a lid, and add half the chopped coriander.

2 Bring the mixture to the boil, reduce the heat, cover and simmer gently for 10 minutes.

3 Stir the mixture occasionally and add a dash of water if the sauce starts to dry out.

4 Ladle the chilli into warmed individual serving bowls, top with the yogurt and garnish with the chopped celery and sliced chilli.

Nutritional information per portion: Energy 309kcal/1302kJ; Protein 16.7g; Carbohydrate 43.7g, of which sugars 14.1g; Fat 8.7g, of which saturates 4.2g; Cholesterol 18mg; Calcium 193mg; Fibre 12.4g; Sodium 1202mg.

Chilli beans with fried eggs and plantain

This extremely quick and delicious meal is made with canned beans for speed. The haricot beans partner well with the lively flavours of the chilli sauce, which gives the beans plenty of fire.

SERVES 6

250ml/8fl oz/1 cup vegetable oil
1 large onion, finely diced
30ml/2 tbsp chilli sauce
1kg/2¼lb/4 cups haricot (navy) beans,
    cooked or canned
1kg/2¼lb/4 cups cooked white rice
6–12 eggs
2 plantains, peeled and sliced
ground black pepper

1 Heat 75ml/5 tbsp of the oil in a non-stick frying pan over medium heat and fry the onion for about 10 minutes until browned.

2 Stir the chilli sauce into the onion, then add the cooked beans and rice. Increase the heat to high and stir-fry the mixture until the rice develops a golden crust. Remove from the heat and leave to stand for 2 minutes.

3 Heat the remaining oil in another pan and fry the plantain slices over medium-high heat for 3 minutes on each side, until they turn a lovely golden colour. Drain and keep warm while you fry the eggs.

4 Scoop a portion of the beans and rice and shape and place on to each plate. Top with the fried eggs and season. Serve with the plantains.

Nutritional information per portion: Energy 777kcal/3267kJ; Protein 29.8g; Carbohydrate 101.2g, of which sugars 12.6g; Fat 31.2g, of which saturates 5.6g; Cholesterol 381mg; Calcium 228mg; Fibre 12.1g; Sodium 796mg.

Pineapple with ginger and chilli

This sweet and fruity dish is very easy to make. The pineapple combines with the tangy flavours of root ginger and fresh chilli to make a sensational accompaniment to complement any meal.

SERVES 4

30ml/2 tbsp groundnut (peanut) oil

2 garlic cloves, finely shredded

40g/1½oz fresh root ginger, peeled
   and finely shredded

2 red Thai chillies, seeded and finely sliced

1 pineapple, trimmed, peeled, cored
   and cut into bitesize chunks

15ml/1 tbsp fish sauce (optional)

30ml/2 tbsp soy sauce

15ml–30ml/1–2 tbsp sugar

30ml/2 tbsp roasted unsalted peanuts,
   finely chopped

1 lime, cut into quarters, to serve

1 Heat a large wok or a large, heavy frying pan and add the groundnut oil. Stir in the garlic, ginger and chillies. Stir-fry for 2 minutes until the ingredients begin to colour.

2 Add the pineapple to the pan and stir-fry for a further 1–2 minutes, until the edges turn golden.

3 Add the fish sauce, if using, and soy sauce to the pan and mix well. Add sugar to taste and continue to stir-fry until the pineapple begins to colour and caramelize.

4 Transfer to a warmed serving dish, sprinkle with the roasted peanuts and serve with lime wedges.

Nutritional information per portion: Energy 185kcal/780kJ; Protein 3g; Carbohydrate 24.1g, of which sugars 23.6g; Fat 9g, of which saturates 1g; Cholesterol 0mg; Calcium 43mg; Fibre 2.9g; Sodium 271mg.

Fruit and vegetables in spicy peanut sauce

An intensely flavoured dish, this classic Indonesian recipe of fruit and vegetables in a fragrant peanut sauce, known as gado gado, can also be a satisfying meal on its own.

SERVES 3–4

corn oil, for deep-frying
500g/1¼lb tofu block, cut into
    4 rectangular pieces
4 shallots, finely sliced
3 carrots, sliced diagonally
12 yard-long beans, cut into
    bitesize pieces
225g/8oz water spinach (kangkung),
    washed and thinly sliced
1 firm mango, pitted (stoned) and cut
    into bitesize chunks
½ pineapple, cored and cut into
    bitesize chunks
225g/8oz mung beansprouts
2 hard-boiled eggs, quartered
salt

FOR THE PEANUT SAUCE

30ml/2 tbsp coconut or groundnut
    (peanut) oil
3 shallots, finely chopped
3 garlic cloves, finely chopped
3–4 fresh red chillies, seeded and
    finely chopped
175g/6oz/1 cup unsalted roasted
    peanuts, finely ground
15g/½oz fresh galangal or root ginger,
    finely chopped
5–10ml/1–2 tsp shrimp paste (optional)
15ml/1 tbsp palm sugar (jaggery)
600ml/1 pint/2½ cups coconut milk
juice of 1 lime
30ml/2 tbsp sweet soy sauce

1 First make the peanut sauce. Heat the oil in a wok or heavy pan, stir in the shallots, garlic and chillies and fry until fragrant and beginning to colour. Add the peanuts, galangal or ginger, shrimp paste, if using, and palm sugar and fry for 4 minutes, until the peanuts begin to darken and ooze a little oil.

2 Pour the coconut milk, lime juice and sweet soy sauce into the pan and bring to the boil. Reduce the heat and simmer gently for 15–20 minutes, until the sauce has reduced a little and thickened. Leave to cool.

3 Heat enough oil in a wok or large pan for deep-frying, add the tofu pieces and fry until golden brown.

4 Using a slotted spoon, remove the cooked tofu pieces from the pan and drain on kitchen paper. Cut the tofu into slices and put aside.

5 Heat 15ml/1 tbsp of the oil from the deep-frying in a small, heavy pan, add the shallots and fry until deep golden in colour. Drain on kitchen paper and put aside.

6 Fill a large pan a third of the way up with water and place a steamer basket over it. Bring the water to the boil and put the carrots and yard-long beans in the basket. Put the lid on, reduce the heat and steam for 3–4 minutes. Add the water spinach to the steamer for a minute, then drain the vegetables and refresh under cold running water.

7 Put the vegetables in a bowl. Add the mango, pineapple and beansprouts and pour in half the peanut sauce. Mix well and transfer to a serving dish. Arrange the egg quarters and tofu slices and drizzle the remaining peanut sauce over the top. Sprinkle with the reserved fried shallots to garnish.

Nutritional information per portion: Energy 449kcal/1873kJ; Protein 22.2g; Carbohydrate 24.5g, of which sugars 20.7g; Fat 30g, of which saturates 5.1g; Cholesterol 108mg; Calcium 611mg; Fibre 5.1g; Sodium 675mg.

Crispy fried tempeh with red chilli and spices

This spicy dish makes a great accompaniment to any main course. Spices and chillies add a sizzle to the delicate flavour of the tempeh. Serve it with cooked rice or stir-fried noodles.

SERVES 3–4

45–60ml/3–4 tbsp coconut or
    groundnut (peanut) oil
500g/1¼lb tempeh or tofu, cut into
    bitesize chunks
4 shallots, finely chopped
4 garlic cloves, finely chopped
25g/1oz fresh galangal or
    fresh root ginger, finely chopped
3–4 red chillies, seeded and
    finely chopped
150ml/¼ pint/⅔ cup sweet soy sauce
30–45ml/2–3 tbsp unsalted
    peanuts, crushed and 1 small bunch
    fresh coriander (cilantro) leaves,
    roughly chopped, to garnish
noodles or rice, to serve

1 Heat 30–45ml/2–3 tbsp of the oil in a wok or large, heavy frying pan. Add the tempeh and stir-fry until golden brown all over. Using a slotted spoon, transfer the tempeh to kitchen paper to drain, then set aside.

2 Wipe the wok or frying pan clean with kitchen paper. Heat the remaining 15ml/1 tbsp oil in the wok or pan, stir in the shallots, garlic, galangal and chillies and fry until fragrant and beginning to colour.

3 Stir in the sweet soy sauce and add the fried tempeh. Stir-fry until the sauce has reduced and is clinging to the tempeh.

4 Transfer the cooked tempeh to a warmed serving dish and sprinkle with the crushed peanuts and chopped coriander leaves. Serve immediately with stir-fried noodles or cooked rice.

Nutritional information per portion: Energy 258kcal/1071kJ; Protein 14.8g; Carbohydrate 7.7g, of which sugars 5.5g; Fat 18.9g, of which saturates 2.6g; Cholesterol 0mg; Calcium 682mg; Fibre 1.7g; Sodium 2680mg.

Tofu in a tangy chilli sauce

Red chilli provides the bite in this light, tasty Vietnamese side dish. This is a very simple way to serve tofu, which can sometimes taste a bit bland, and the dish looks delicious too.

SERVES 4

vegetable or groundnut (peanut) oil,
    for deep-frying
450g/1lb firm tofu, rinsed and cut
    into bitesize cubes
4 shallots, finely sliced
1 Thai chilli, seeded and chopped
25g/1oz fresh root ginger, peeled
    and finely chopped
4 garlic cloves, finely chopped
6 large ripe tomatoes, skinned, seeded
    and finely chopped
30ml/2 tbsp soy sauce
10ml/2 tsp sugar
ground black pepper
mint leaves and strips of red chilli,
    to garnish

1 Heat enough oil for deep-frying in a wok or heavy pan. Fry the cubes of tofu, in batches, until crisp and golden. Remove each batch as it is done with a slotted spoon and drain on kitchen paper.

2 When the tofu is cooked, pour off most of the oil, reserving 30ml/2 tbsp in the wok. Add the shallots, chilli, ginger and garlic and stir-fry until they are fragrant. Stir in the tomatoes, soy sauce and sugar.

3 Reduce the heat and simmer for 10–15 minutes until the liquid ingredients form a sauce. Stir in 105ml/7 tbsp water and bring to the boil.

4 Season the sauce with a little pepper to taste and return the tofu to the pan. Mix well and simmer gently for 2–3 minutes to heat through. Garnish with mint leaves and chilli strips and serve immediately.

Nutritional information per portion: Energy 423kcal/1749kJ; Protein 17.9g; Carbohydrate 7.8g, of which sugars 4.5g; Fat 35.8g, of which saturates 5.3g; Cholesterol 0mg; Calcium 607mg; Fibre 2.8g; Sodium 296mg.

Sweet chilli rice with sour chickpeas

Contrasting flavours can be just as interesting as complementary ones. Chickpeas, spiced with plenty of chillies and soured with lemon juice, taste remarkably good with sweet rice.

SERVES 6

225g/8oz tomatoes, skinned
350g/12oz/2 cups dried chickpeas, soaked overnight
60ml/4 tbsp vegetable oil
1 large onion, very finely chopped
15ml/1 tbsp ground coriander
15ml/1 tbsp ground cumin
5ml/1 tsp ground fenugreek
5ml/1 tsp ground cinnamon
1–2 fresh green chillies, seeded and thinly sliced
2.5cm/1in piece fresh root ginger, peeled and grated
60ml/4 tbsp lemon juice

15ml/1 tbsp chopped fresh coriander (cilantro)
salt and ground black pepper

FOR THE RICE
40g/1½oz/3 tbsp butter
4 green cardamom pods
4 cloves
350g/12oz/1¾ cups basmati rice, soaked for 30 minutes and drained
650ml/22fl oz/2¾ cups boiling water
5–10ml/1–2 tsp sugar
5–6 saffron threads, soaked in warm water

1 Chop the skinned tomatoes. Set aside. Drain the chickpeas into a large pan. Cover with water, bring to the boil, cover and simmer, for 1–1¼ hours. Drain, reserving the cooking liquid.

2 Heat the oil in a pan. Reserve 30ml/2 tbsp of the onion and add the remainder to the pan. Cook over medium heat for about 4–5 minutes, stirring. Add the tomatoes. Cook over low heat for about 5 minutes, stirring, until soft.

3 Stir in the ground coriander, cumin, fenugreek and cinnamon. Cook for 30 seconds, then add the chickpeas and 350ml/12fl oz/1½ cups of the reserved cooking liquid. Season with salt, then cover and simmer gently for 15–20 minutes. Add more liquid if needed.

4 Melt the butter for the rice in a pan and fry the cardamom pods and cloves for 30 seconds. Add the rice, stir well, then pour in the boiling water. Cover tightly and simmer for 10 minutes, then turn off the heat and stir in the sugar and saffron liquid. Cover. Add the reserved chopped onion, chillies, ginger, lemon juice, and coriander to the chickpeas. Serve with the rice.

Nutritional information per portion: Energy 556kcal/2327kJ; Protein 18.2g; Carbohydrate 84.6g, of which sugars 8.2g; Fat 16.8g, of which saturates 4.7g; Cholesterol 14mg; Calcium 130mg; Fibre 7.6g; Sodium 70mg.

Spiced rice

This aromatic rice makes a good alternative to the plain steamed version. A variety of spices are included – chilli for fire, turmeric for colour and coriander for its wonderful, cooling flavour.

SERVES 4

15ml/1 tbsp vegetable oil

2–3 green or red Thai chillies, seeded
   and finely chopped

2 garlic cloves, finely chopped

2.5cm/1in piece fresh root
   ginger, chopped

5ml/1 tsp sugar

10–15ml/2–3 tsp ground turmeric

225g/8oz/generous 1 cup long
   grain rice

30ml/2 tbsp soy sauce

600ml/1 pint/2¹/₂ cups water or stock

1 bunch of fresh coriander (cilantro),
   stalks removed, leaves finely chopped

salt and ground black pepper

1 Heat the oil in a frying pan. Stir in the chillies, garlic and ginger with the sugar. As the spices begin to colour, stir in the ground turmeric.

2 Add the rice, coating it well, then pour in the soy sauce and the water or stock – the liquid should sit about 2.5cm/1in above the rice. Season with salt and pepper and bring the liquid to the boil.

3 Reduce the heat and cover the pan, and then simmer for about 25 minutes, or until the water has all been absorbed. Remove from the heat and leave the rice to steam for a further 10 minutes.

4 Transfer the rice on to a serving dish. Add some of the coriander and toss together using a fork. Garnish with the remaining coriander.

Nutritional information per portion: Energy 404kcal/1686kJ; Protein 24.8g; Carbohydrate 35g, of which sugars 4g; Fat 18.3g, of which saturates 3.8g; Cholesterol 251mg; Calcium 38mg; Fibre 2.2g; Sodium 93mg.

Chilli vegetable rice

This exquisite dish of spiced rice can be adapted to include all kinds of savoury ingredients. The heat of the chillies merge with the other flavourings to give a wonderfully delectable result.

SERVES 4

200g/7oz/1 cup jasmine rice
2 yard-long beans or 5 green beans
¼ cucumber
2 hard-boiled eggs
3 fresh red chillies, seeded
   and chopped
4 lime leaves, finely shredded
5ml/1 tsp salt
1.5ml/¼ tsp ground black pepper
30ml/2 tbsp fresh lime juice
2 tomatoes, chopped

1 Put the rice in a sieve (strainer), rinse under cold running water until the water runs clear, then put it in a pan and cover with water up to 4cm/1½in above the rice. Cook for 12–15 minutes until tender.

2 Blanch the beans in a pan of boiling water for 2 minutes. Drain, cool and dice the beans finely. Peel the cucumber and cut it in half. Carefully scrape out the seeds and discard, then finely chop the remaining flesh into cubes.

3 Remove the shells from the eggs, and chop the hard-boiled eggs into small pieces. Toss all the ingredients together in a large bowl and serve.

Nutritional information per portion: Energy 199kcal/834kJ; Protein 4.6g; Carbohydrate 43.4g, of which sugars 6.6g; Fat 0.7g, of which saturates 0.1g; Cholesterol 105mg; Calcium 23mg; Fibre 1.6g; Sodium 232mg.

Potatoes baked with tomatoes and chilli

The flavour of this comforting potato dish is enlivened when cooked with chillies and other spices. Hot and fiery potatoes make a fabulous accompaniment to meat, poultry or fish.

SERVES 4–6

675g/1½lb new potatoes
15ml/1 tbsp butter
45ml/3 tbsp olive oil
2 red onions, halved lengthways,
    halved again crossways, and sliced
    along the grain
3–4 garlic cloves, chopped
5–10ml/1–2 tsp cumin seeds, crushed
1 fresh red chilli, seeded and chopped

10ml/2 tsp dried oregano
10ml/2 tsp sugar
15ml/1 tbsp white wine vinegar
400g/14oz can chopped tomatoes,
    drained of juice
12–16 black olives
115g/4oz feta cheese, crumbled
salt and ground black pepper
1 lemon, cut into wedges

1 Preheat the oven to 200°C/400°F/Gas 6. Cook the potatoes for 15–20 minutes, until tender. Drain and refresh in cold water. Peel and cut the potatoes into thick slices or bitesize wedges.

2 Heat the butter and 30ml/2 tbsp of the oil in a heavy pan, stir in the onions and garlic and cook until soft. Add the cumin seeds, chopped chilli and most of the oregano, then add the sugar, vinegar and tomatoes and mix well. Season with salt and pepper.

3 Put the potatoes and olives into a baking dish and top with the tomato mixture. Crumble the feta cheese evenly over the top and sprinkle with the remaining oregano.

4 Generously drizzle with the remaining oil, then bake in the preheated oven for 25–30 minutes. Serve hot, straight from the oven, with lemon wedges to squeeze over.

Nutritional information per portion: Energy 243kcal/1016kJ; Protein 6.3g; Carbohydrate 27.5g, of which sugars 9.3g; Fat 12.8g, of which saturates 5g; Cholesterol 19mg; Calcium 102mg; Fibre 2.9g; Sodium 447mg.

Andean spiced potatoes

*This version of the classic Andean stew combines potatoes, fresh cheese and hot chilli sauce.
There are many variations but these three main ingredients are always included.*

SERVES 6

1kg/2¹/₄lb floury potatoes, such as
  King Edward
60ml/4 tbsp vegetable oil
6 spring onions (scallions), chopped
5ml/1 tsp grated garlic
30ml/2 tbsp chilli sauce
5ml/1 tsp paprika
250ml/8fl oz/1 cup evaporated milk
120ml/4fl oz/¹/₂ cup water
150g/5oz feta cheese
4 hard-boiled eggs, roughly chopped
salt and ground black pepper

1 Boil the potatoes in their skins in lightly salted water for 20 minutes, until
tender. Peel them and crush lightly (they do not need to be mashed to a
purée). Set aside.

2 Heat the oil in a frying pan over medium heat and fry the spring onions
and garlic for about 8 minutes, until browned. Add the chilli sauce and
paprika, season, then stir in the cooked potatoes, milk and water.

3 Mash the cheese with a fork and add to the potato mixture with the
chopped eggs. Stir with a spoon and simmer for 5 minutes before serving.

Nutritional information per portion: Energy 306kcal/1281kJ; Protein 11.6g; Carbohydrate 28.7g, of which sugars 2.8g;
Fat 17.1g, of which saturates 5.5g; Cholesterol 144mg; Calcium 129mg; Fibre 1.8g; Sodium 427mg.

Broad bean, potato and chilli cheese salad

Chillies do not need to dominate to make their presence felt in this distinctively spicy salad. It can be made with fresh or frozen beans, but fresh young beans have the best texture.

SERVES 4

250g/9oz small white potatoes

250g/9oz/2 cups shelled broad (fava) beans

kernels of 1 fresh corn on the cob or 1 medium can corn in unsalted water

150g/5oz feta cheese, cut into 1cm/¹/₂in dice

15ml/1 tbsp white wine vinegar

45ml/3 tbsp olive oil

1 fresh red or green chilli, seeded and finely chopped

salt and ground black pepper

1 Boil the potatoes in lightly salted water for 20 minutes, until tender. Drain and allow to cool for 10 minutes, then gently slide the skin off with your fingers and cut into 1cm/¹/₂in cube.

2 Boil the beans in lightly salted water for 15 minutes. Drain and allow to cool, then pop them out of their skins. If the beans are young and small you need not do this. If using fresh corn on the cob, boil for 10 minutes, then drain and slice off the kernels with a knife. If using canned corn, drain it.

3 Mix the cooked potatoes, beans and corn kernels with the diced feta cheese in a large salad bowl and dress with the vinegar, oil, salt and pepper. Sprinkle the chilli on top and serve.

Nutritional information per portion: Energy 293kcal/1225kJ; Protein 12.6g; Carbohydrate 24.6g, of which sugars 4.6g; Fat 16.7g, of which saturates 6.5g; Cholesterol 26mg; Calcium 175mg; Fibre 5g; Sodium 620mg.

Potatoes in hot peanut sauce

Six green chillies provide plenty of heat in this simple recipe of boiled potatoes with a piquant peanut sauce. It can be cooked quickly with ingredients you may already have in your pantry.

SERVES 6

500g/1¼lb white potatoes
75ml/5 tbsp vegetable oil
250g/9oz red onion, finely chopped
250g/9oz/2 cups shelled peanuts, ground
salt
3 hard-boiled eggs, quartered, lettuce
leaves, and sections of cooked corn on
the cob (optional) to serve

FOR THE CHILLI SAUCE

6 green chillies, sliced in half and seeded
5ml/1 tbsp vegetable oil
½ chopped red onion
2 chopped garlic cloves
salt

1 To make the chilli sauce, fry the green chillies in vegetable oil with the onion and garlic cloves until the onion is soft. Season. Remove from the heat and purée in a blender or food processor. Set aside.

2 Boil the potatoes in lightly salted water for about 25 minutes, until tender. Remove from the heat, drain and peel. Keep them warm. Heat the oil in a frying pan and fry the onion for about 10 minutes until it starts to caramelize.

3 Add the chilli sauce and the peanuts and cook for 2–3 minutes, stirring, until all the ingredients are fragrant and have released their flavours. Add more vegetable oil if the sauce becomes too thick. Remove from the heat.

4 Lay one or two lettuce leaves on each plate. Slice the potatoes and pile them in the centre. Pour the sauce over the potatoes and add two quarters of egg, and sections of corn on the cob if using.

Nutritional information per portion: Energy 432kcal/1799kJ; Protein 15.8g; Carbohydrate 23.1g, of which sugars 7.2g; Fat 31.4g, of which saturates 5.2g; Cholesterol 95mg; Calcium 56mg; Fibre 4.1g; Sodium 102mg.

Stir-fried spinach with chilli

This sizzling salad combines fresh water spinach and lots of chilli to make a delightfully spicy accompaniment to meat or fish. This is a lovely way to enjoy water spinach.

SERVES 4–6

2 garlic cloves
2 red or green chillies
30ml/2 tbsp groundnut (peanut) oil
500g/1¼lb fresh water spinach
45ml/3 tbsp chilli sauce
salt and ground black pepper

1 Peel the garlic cloves and finely chop. Slice the chillies in half, carefully remove the seeds, and then finely chop.

2 Heat a wok or large pan and add the groundnut oil. Stir in the garlic and chillies, and stir-fry for 1 minute.

3 Add the water spinach and toss around the pan so the spinach is coated well in the chillies.

4 Once the spinach leaves begin to wilt, add the chilli sauce. Season to taste with salt and pepper and serve immediately.

Nutritional information per portion: Energy 120kcal/500kJ; Protein 3g; Carbohydrate 5g, of which sugars 3g; Fat 10g, of which saturates 2g; Cholesterol 0mg; Calcium 36mg; Fibre 3.3g; Sodium 200mg.

Green leaf and chilli salad

A delicious accompaniment to grilled seafood dishes, this lively salad combines crunchy salad leaves, leeks and onion while the sharp spiciness of chillies provides a refreshing edge.

SERVES 2–3

250g/9oz green salad leaves
115g/4oz leeks, finely sliced
1 white onion, finely sliced
2 green chillies, seeded and finely sliced
1 red chilli, seeded and finely sliced
15ml/1 tbsp sesame seeds, to garnish

FOR THE DRESSING
5ml/1 tsp pine nuts, ground
15ml/1 tbsp chilli powder
5ml/1 tsp sesame oil
1 garlic clove, crushed
30ml/2 tbsp light soy sauce
30ml/2 tbsp water

1 Tear the salad leaves into bitesize pieces. Mix the leeks, onion and green and red chillies.

2 For the salad dressing, mix the pine nuts with the chilli powder, sesame oil, garlic, soy sauce and water in a bowl.

3 Stir the dressing gently, allowing the flavours to mingle, and then add the chillies, onions and leeks.

4 Place the green leaves in a salad bowl and pour over the dressing. Toss the salad, garnish with the sesame seeds and serve.

Nutritional information per portion: Energy 54kcal/224kJ; Protein 2.5g; Carbohydrate 4.1g, of which sugars 4g; Fat 3.2g, of which saturates 0.4g; Cholesterol 0mg; Calcium 58mg; Fibre 1.7g; Sodium 719mg.

Spicy pak choi with lime dressing

Beware, as this pretty vegetable dish is extremely hot! The cool and creamy coconut dressing is intensely flavoured with plenty of red chilli, resulting in a wonderful and tangy dish.

SERVES 4

15ml/1 tbsp sunflower oil

3 fresh red chillies, thinly sliced

4 garlic cloves, thinly sliced

6 spring onions (scallions),
    sliced diagonally

2 pak choi (bok choy), shredded

15ml/1 tbsp crushed peanuts

FOR THE DRESSING

30ml/2 tbsp fresh lime juice

15–30ml/1–2 tbsp fish sauce or
    mushroom sauce

250ml/8fl oz/1 cup reduced-fat
    coconut milk

1 Make the dressing. Put the lime juice and fish sauce or mushroom sauce in a bowl and mix well, then gradually whisk in the coconut milk until combined.

2 Heat the oil in a wok or large pan and stir-fry the chillies for 2–3 minutes, until crisp. Transfer to a plate using a slotted spoon. Add the garlic to the wok and stir-fry until golden brown. Transfer to the plate.

3 Stir-fry the white parts of the spring onions for 2 minutes, then add the green parts and stir-fry for 1 minute more. Transfer to the plate.

4 Bring a pan of lightly salted water to the boil and add the pak choi. Stir twice, then drain immediately. Place the pak choi in a bowl, add the dressing and toss to mix. Sprinkle with the crushed peanuts and the chilli mixture. Serve warm or cold.

Nutritional information per portion: Energy 58kcal/244kJ; Protein 2.2g; Carbohydrate 5g, of which sugars 4.8g; Fat 3.5g, of which saturates 0.5g; Cholesterol 0mg; Calcium 113mg; Fibre 1.4g; Sodium 408mg.

Egg, watercress and chilli salad

Chillies and eggs may seem unlikely partners, but actually work very well together. The fresh peppery flavour of the watercress makes the perfect foundation for this tasty salad.

SERVES 2

15ml/1 tbsp groundnut
   (peanut) oil
1 garlic clove, thinly sliced
4 eggs
2 shallots, thinly sliced
2 small fresh red chillies, seeded
   and thinly sliced
1/2 small cucumber, finely diced

1cm/1/2in piece fresh root ginger,
   peeled and grated
juice of 2 limes
30ml/2 tbsp soy sauce
5ml/1 tsp caster (superfine) sugar
small bunch coriander (cilantro)
bunch watercress or rocket (arugula),
   coarsely chopped

1 Heat the oil in a frying pan. Add the sliced garlic and cook over low heat until the garlic starts to turn golden.

2 Crack the eggs into the pan. Break the yolks with a wooden spatula, then fry until the eggs are almost firm. Remove from the pan and set aside.

3 Put the shallots, chillies, cucumber and ginger into a large bowl and mix together until well blended.

4 In a separate bowl, whisk the lime juice with the soy sauce and sugar. Pour this dressing over the vegetables and toss lightly.

5 Set aside a few coriander sprigs for the garnish. Chop the rest and add it to the salad. Toss it again so it is thoroughly mixed.

6 Reserve a few watercress or rocket sprigs and arrange the remainder on two serving plates. Cut the fried eggs into slices and divide them between the watercress or rocket mounds.

7 Spoon the shallot mixture over the eggs and serve immediately, garnished with the reserved coriander and watercress or rocket.

Nutritional information per portion: Energy 215kcal/894kJ; Protein 14.2g; Carbohydrate 2.4g, of which sugars 2.2g; Fat 16.9g, of which saturates 4.2g; Cholesterol 381mg; Calcium 112mg; Fibre 0.8g; Sodium 1223mg.

Feta, chilli and parsley salad

This simple and refreshing salad only uses one chilli which is just enough to accentuate the flavour of the milder ingredients. Add more chillies if you want to enjoy more heat.

SERVES 3–4

2 red onions, cut in half lengthways and
    finely sliced along the grain
1 green (bell) pepper, seeded and sliced
1 fresh green chilli, seeded and chopped
2–3 garlic cloves, chopped
1 bunch of fresh flat leaf parsley,
    roughly chopped
225g/8oz firm feta cheese, grated
2 large tomatoes, skinned, seeded
    and finely chopped
30–45ml/2–3 tbsp olive oil
salt and ground black pepper
paprika, to garnish

1 Sprinkle the onions with a little salt to draw out the moisture. Leave for about 10 minutes, then rinse and pat dry with kitchen paper.

2 Put the red onions and green pepper into a bowl. Add the chilli, garlic, flat leaf parsley, feta cheese and tomatoes. Gently mix together.

3 Add the olive oil and salt and pepper and toss gently, ensuring that all the ingredients are mixed together well and coated in the olive oil.

4 Transfer the mixed salad on to a large serving dish with a sprinkling of the paprika on top, and serve.

Nutritional information per portion: Energy 253kcal/1049kJ; Protein 11.1g; Carbohydrate 13.4g, of which sugars 11g; Fat 17.6g, of which saturates 8.6g; Cholesterol 39mg; Calcium 260mg; Fibre 3.2g; Sodium 824mg.

Red hot mango salad

Strips of seaweed and tomatoes are combined with the mango to create a unique and tangy dish, while chilli oil provides the fire. Serve this spicy salad with grilled meats and fish.

SERVES 4

50g/2oz fine thread seaweed, reconstituted in water, or 225g/8oz fresh seaweed, cut into strips
1 green mango, grated
2–3 ripe tomatoes, skinned, seeded and chopped
4–6 spring onions (scallions), white parts only, sliced
25g/1oz fresh root ginger, grated
45ml/3 tbsp coconut or cane vinegar
10ml/2 tsp chilli oil
15ml/1 tbsp sugar
salt and ground black pepper

1 Bring a large pan of water to the boil, drop in the seaweed, remove from the heat and leave to soak for 15 minutes. Drain and refresh under cold running water. Using your hands, squeeze the seaweed dry.

2 Put the seaweed, mango, tomatoes, spring onions and ginger into a bowl and mix to combine.

3 In a separate bowl, mix together the coconut or cane vinegar, chilli oil and sugar, stirring until the sugar has completely dissolved. Pour the dressing over the salad, toss together so everything is covered well in the chilli and sugar mixture. Season with salt and pepper to taste and serve.

Nutritional information per portion: Energy 75kcal/315kJ; Protein 2.4g; Carbohydrate 12g, of which sugars 11.8g; Fat 2.2g, of which saturates 0.3g; Cholesterol 0mg; Calcium 110mg; Fibre 2.8g; Sodium 85mg.

Spicy fruit salad in a tangy dressing

Designed to be flexible, this refreshing salad, tossed in a pungent and zesty dressing, can include any choice of fruit and vegetables, so you can make this as tropical as you like.

SERVES 4–6

1 green mango, finely sliced

1 ripe, firm papaya, finely sliced

1–2 star fruit (carambola), finely sliced

1/2 pineapple, finely sliced and cut into
    bitesize pieces

1/2 pomelo, segmented

1 small cucumber, roughly peeled, seeded
    and finely sliced

1 jicama, finely sliced

a handful of beansprouts, to garnish

FOR THE SAUCE

10ml/2 tsp shrimp paste

225g/8oz/1 1/2 cups roasted peanuts

4 garlic cloves, chopped

2–4 fresh red chillies, seeded
    and chopped

15ml/1 tbsp tamarind paste

30ml/2 tbsp palm sugar (jaggery)

salt

1 To make the sauce, dry-fry the shrimp paste in a small, heavy frying pan until it is golden and emits a toasted aroma.

2 Using a mortar and pestle or a processor or blender, pound the peanuts, garlic and chillies to a coarse paste. Beat in the dry-fried shrimp paste, tamarind paste and sugar. Add enough water to make a thick pouring sauce, then stir until the sugar has dissolved. Season the sauce with salt to taste.

3 Put all the fruit and vegetables, except the beansprouts, into a large bowl. Pour in some of the sauce and toss gently together so most of the fruit and vegetables are coated in the sauce. Leave the salad to stand for 30 minutes.

4 Transfer the salad into a large serving dish or four to six individual serving bowls. Sprinkle the beansprouts over the top. Then drizzle the remaining sauce over the top and serve.

Nutritional information per portion: Energy 321kcal/1344kJ; Protein 12.3g; Carbohydrate 30g, of which sugars 27.2g; Fat 17.7g, of which saturates 3.3g; Cholesterol 8mg; Calcium 91mg; Fibre 6.2g; Sodium 81mg.

Chilli basics

This section features an extensive,

illlustrated guide to the many types of

chillies and chilli products available,

and includes useful tips to help you

select and store them. There are also

step-by-step instructions for basic

cooking techniques, from preparing

and roasting chillies to making chilli

powder and a decorative chilli flower.

The chilli family

There are over two hundred different types of chilli, which are all part of the nightshade (Solanacae) family, like tomatoes and potatoes. Most of those used for culinary purposes belong to the genus Capsicum annuum.

These chillies were originally thought to be annuals, which explains the name, but can be perennial when cultivated in the tropics. The plants grow to a height of 1m/1yd, and chillies of this type include jalapeños, cayennes, Anaheim chillies and poblanos, as well as (bell) peppers.

Tabasco chillies and the very hot Punjab chillies belong to a group called *Capsicum frutescens*, while Scotch bonnets and habaneros – the fragrant hot chillies that look like tam-o'-shanters – are *Capsicum chinense*. Some of the largest chilli plants are *Capsicum baccatum*. Ajis fall into this category, as do peri-peri chillies. Finally, there is a small group

BELOW: *Chillies are members of the nightshade* (Solanacae) *family, like tomatoes and potatoes.*

called *Capsicum pubescens*. The most notable chilli in this group is the manzano. The name means 'apple', and these chillies resemble crab apples in size and shape.

Unless you grow chillies or are lucky enough to live near a farmer's market that stock these flavoursome ingredients, you are unlikely to encounter more than a few of the more common varieties, such as serranos, jalapeños and cayennes, and even these may not be identified as such. Supermarkets have a habit of limiting their labelling to the obvious, like 'red chillies' or – 'hot red chillies'.

This raises other issues. How do you know whether a chilli is hot or not? Are small chillies hotter than big ones? Or red chillies hotter than green? The answer to the last two questions is no. Although some of the world's hottest chillies are tiny, there are some large varieties that are real scorchers. Colour isn't an infallible indicator either. Most chillies start out green and ripen to red, but some start yellow and become red, and yet others start yellow and stay yellow, and across the spectrum you'll find hot varieties.

Fortunately for those of us who like to have some warning as to whether the contents of our shopping basket will be fragrant or fiery, there are rating systems for the heat in chillies. The best known of these grades

ABOVE: Capsicum chinense *is the genus in which fragrant hot chillies such as habaneros are included.*

chillies in Scoville units. Until relatively recently, the world's hottest chilli was reckoned to be the Mexican red savina habanero, which scores 557,000 units on the Scoville scale, but a new contender, the tezpur chilli, has been discovered in India. The tezpur registers a blistering 855,000 Scoville units, and is so hot that it is said to have triggered heart attacks in the unwary or novice taster.

Scoville units are useful when it comes to fine comparisons such as these, but working with units measured in this way can be unwieldy. For general classification, a simpler system, which rates chillies out of ten, is more often used.

BELOW: *Chillies can be fresh, dried, preserved in oil and ground into powders.*

TYPES OF CHILLI

You will find both fresh and dried chillies on sale. Dried chillies can be stored like other spices, and can be rehydrated with excellent results. Some chillies actually taste better when they have been dried. It is well worth getting to know as many different varieties as possible. Then, like a true aficionado, you can start blending several types for the ultimate in chilli pleasure.

The following descriptions of chillies are listed by their heat scale, with 10 being the hottest.

Anaheim

Heat scale 2–3: Their alternative name of 'California long green' gives some idea of what these large chillies look like (they are also known as 'New Mexico'). The pods are about 15cm/6in long and about 5cm/2in wide, making them good candidates for stuffing. The flavour is fresh and fruity, like a cross between tart apples and green (bell) peppers. Anaheim skins can be a bit tough, so these chillies are best roasted and peeled. The dried chillies are used to make a mild chilli powder.

ABOVE:
Anaheim chilli

BELOW:
Ancho chillies

Ancho

Heat scale 3: Dried poblanos, these are larger than most other dried chillies. Open the packet and savour the wonderful fruity aroma – like dates or dried figs. After rehydration, anchos can be stuffed, and they also taste great sliced or chopped in stir-fries and similar dishes.

Guajillo

Heat scale 3: These dried chillies are about 15cm/6in long, with rough skin. The mature fresh pods are a deep reddish brown and have a smooth texture. It is thought they might be related to Anaheim chillies, as they look similar. They have a mild, slightly bitter flavour, suggestive of green tea. Guajillos are used in many classic salsas.

ABOVE: *Guajillo chillies*

Italia

Heat scale 3: Juicy and refreshing, these dark green chillies ripen to a rich, dark red. They taste great in salads and have an affinity for tropical fruit, especially mangoes.

BELOW:
Mulato chillies

Mulato

Heat scale 3: A dried chilli with a thin, wrinkled, dark brown skin, this is related to the ancho. The flavour is smoky and herby.

Poblano

Heat scale 3: Big and beautiful, poblanos look like sweet (bell) peppers, and are perfect for stuffing. They start off a deep green and ripen to a bright, clear red or rich, dark brown. The flavour is spicier than that of a sweet pepper, with peachy overtones. Poblanos taste wonderful with other chillies, whose flavour they appear to boost.

BELOW:
Poblano chillies

ABOVE:
Pasado chillies

Pasado

Heat scale 3–4: Very dark brown, skinny, dried chillies, these are generally about 10cm/4in long. When rehydrated, they taste lemony, with a hint of cucumber and apple. Pasados have an affinity for black beans, and make a fine salsa.

BELOW: *Cascabel chillies*

Cascabel

Heat scale 4: The name translates as 'little rattle', and refers to the sound the seeds make inside this round dried chilli. The woody, nutty flavour is best appreciated when the skin is removed. Soak them, then either scrape the flesh off the skin or sieve (strain) it. Cascabels are great in stews, soups and salsas.

Cherry Hot

Heat scale 4: Pungent, with thick walls, these chillies look like large versions of the fruit for which they are named. The skins can be tough, so they are best peeled. Cherry hot chillies have a sweetish flavour and make good pickles.

BELOW: *Cherry hot chillies*

Costeno Amarillo

Heat scale 4: Not to be confused with the much hotter aji amarillo, this is a pale orange dried chilli, which is ideal for use in yellow salsas and Mexican mole sauce. It has a citrus tang and is used to give depth to the flavour of soups and stews.

Pasilla

Heat scale 4: The first thing you notice is their rich liquorice aroma. Quite large at about 15cm/6in in length, pasillas have a spicy, fruity flavour that is good with shellfish, sauces and mushrooms.

ABOVE:
Pasilla chillies

ABOVE: *Fresno chillies*

Fresno

Heat scale 5: Plump and cylindrical, with tapered ends, these fresh chillies are most often sold red, although you will sometimes find green or yellow ones in the supermarkets. They look rather similar to jalapeños, and can be substituted for them if necessary.

Cultivating Chillies

If you can grow tomatoes, then you'll be able to try your luck with chillies. They enjoy similar conditions, prefer higher temperatures, need watering more often and like slightly acid soils. You can grow them in tubs, hanging baskets or pots on the windowsill. Raise the plants under glass in spring, or buy them from a good plant nursery. Plant out when frost is no longer a problem and the first flowers are visible. Water well in dry weather, mulch thickly and feed fortnightly with a high-potash fertilizer. Stake taller varieties. Pinch out growing tips if sideshoots are not being made and stop these once they have set fruit. During the growing season, watch for aphids, cutworms or slugs, and treat. Harvest about 12–16 weeks after planting out. Pull up plants and hang under glass in a sunny place when frost threatens to encourage the fruit to continue ripening.

ABOVE:
Jalapeno chillies

Jalapeño

Heat scale 4–7: These are frequently
seen in supermarkets. Plump and
stubby, like fat fingers, they have
shiny skins. They are sold at the green
and the red stage, although the
former seem to be marginally more
popular. Jalapeños have a piquant,
grassy flavour, and are widely used in
salsas, salads, dips and stews; they are
also canned and bottled. Their fame is
due to the fact that they are the best
known and most commonly used
chilli in Mexican food. A heat-free
jalapeño has been developed in the
US. Too thick-skinned to be sun-dried,
jalapeños are generally smoke-dried
and acquire a name
change. In this form
they are known as
chipotle chillies.

BELOW:
*Pickled
jalapeño
chillies*

Hungarian Wax

Heat scale 5: These really do
look waxy, like novelty
candles. Unlike many chillies,
they start off yellow, not green. It is
not necessary to peel them, and they
are often used in salads and salsas.

Aji Amarillo

Heat scale 6–7: There are several
different varieties of this chilli,
including one that is yellow when
fully ripe, and a large brown aji that is
frequently dried. The chillies average
about 10cm/4in in length and look
rather like miniature windsocks. Red
ajis originated in Peru, and were
popular among the Incas.

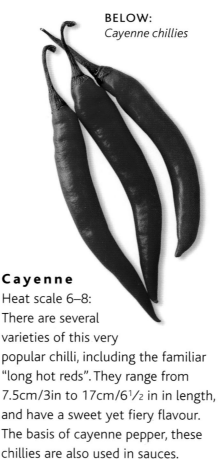

BELOW:
Cayenne chillies

Cayenne

Heat scale 6–8:
There are several
varieties of this very
popular chilli, including the familiar
"long hot reds". They range from
7.5cm/3in to 17cm/6$\frac{1}{2}$ in in length,
and have a sweet yet fiery flavour.
The basis of cayenne pepper, these
chillies are also used in sauces.

ABOVE:
*Chipotle
chillies*

Chipotle

Heat scale 6–10: This smoke-dried
jalapeño has wrinkled, dark red skin
and thick flesh. Chipotles need long,
slow cooking to soften them and
bring out their full flavour, which is
hot and tasty with a deep smokiness.

Serrano

Heat scale 7: Usually sold green, these
are small (about 4cm/1$\frac{1}{2}$in long) and
quite slender. Serranos are the classic
Mexican green chilli (chiles verdes).
The flavour is clean and crisp, with a
suggestion of citrus. Serranos are
thin-skinned and do not
need to be peeled.
They dry well but
are seldom
sold that
way.

ABOVE:
*Serrano
chillies*

ABOVE: *Bird's eye chillies*

Bird's Eye

Heat scale 8: Small and extremely hot, these come from a highly volatile family of chillies that are found in Africa, Asia, the United States and the Caribbean, and often labelled simply as 'Thai chillies'. Thin-fleshed and explosively hot, they are sold green and red, often with the stems still attached. Dried, they are available in jars. They are called bird's eyes because they are liked by mynah birds.

ABOVE: *Dried bird's eye chillies*

Tiny Terrors

Thailand grows many different varieties of chillies. The smallest are so tiny they are popularly referred to as prik kee noo (mouse droppings). Use cautiously as they are fiery hot.

De Arbol

Heat scale 8: More often sold dried than fresh, these smooth cayenne-type chillies are slim and curvacious. A warm orange-red, they are about 7.5cm/3in long. De arbols combine blistering heat with a clean, grassy flavour. Add them to soups or use to enliven vinegar or oil. Unlike most dried chillies, which must be soaked in hot water for 20–30 minutes before use, dry de arbol pods can be crumbled and added straight to stews or similar dishes. To reduce the heat, slit them and shake out the seeds first.

LEFT: *Dried de arbol chillies*

Manzano

Heat scale 9: This delicious chilli is very hot and fruity. About the size of a crab apple, it is the only chilli to have purple/black seeds.

Habanero

Heat scale 10: Don't imagine that intense heat is the only defining feature of this lantern-shaped chilli. Habaneros have a wonderful, fruity flavour, and a surprisingly delicate aroma. Some say it reminds them of chardonnay wine; others that it is redolent of sun-warmed apricots. Don't sniff them too enthusiastically, however, and be ultra-cautious when

ABOVE: *Dried habanero chillies*

handling habaneros, for they are excessively hot. Always wear thick gloves when preparing them, and don't stand over a food processor or blender when using them to make a paste, or the fumes may burn your face. When cooking with habaneros, a little goes a long way. They are very good with fruit and in salsas. Dried habaneros have medium-thick flesh and wrinkled skins. When rehydrated, they have a rich tropical-fruit flavour.

Scotch Bonnets

Heat scale 10: Often confused with habaneros, which they closely resemble, Scotch bonnets are grown in Jamaica and are the principal ingredient of jerk seasoning. Use Scotch bonnets very cautiously as they are one of the hottest chillies. It is advisable to deseed them before use unless you can tolerate their intense and lingering flavour.

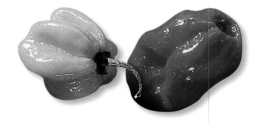

ABOVE: *Scotch bonnet chillies*

Chilli products

Specialist stores, devoted to chillies and chilli products, are springing up all over the world. Alongside mugs, plates, bowls and aprons rioting with chilli motifs, you'll find an astonishing array of powders, pastes, sauces and oils.

Powders

Anything connected with chillies tends to be confusing, and chilli powder is no exception. The name suggests that this product is simply powdered chilli, but it is in fact a blend of several ingredients, designed specifically for making chilli con carne. In addition to ground hot chillies, it typically contains cumin, oregano, salt and garlic powder.

BELOW: *Ancho powder*

ABOVE: *Chilli powder*

RIGHT: *Pasilla powder*

ABOVE: *Paprika*

BELOW: *Cayenne pepper*

Pure powders – the whole chilli and nothing but the chilli – are less easy to come by, but are available from specialist stores and the Internet. Ancho, caribe and Anaheim (New Mexico) red powders are mild (heat scale 3). Pasilla, a rich, dark powder, registers 4 on the heat scale, while chipotle is a little hotter still.

Cayenne pepper is a very fine ground powder from the *Capsicum frutescens* variety of chilli. The placenta (the fibrous white inner lining) and seeds are included, so it is very hot. Tiny amounts of cayenne are often added to cheese and egg dishes, and it is sprinkled over smoked fish and prawns (shrimp). It is also added to some curries.

Paprika is a fine, rich red powder made from mild chillies. The core and seeds are removed, but the flavour can still be quite pungent. Hungarians have adopted this as their national spice, but it is also widely used in Spanish and Portuguese cooking. Look out for pimentón dulce, a delicious smoked paprika from Spain.

Convenient Chillies

Jars of whole chillies in white wine vinegar are handy. Also look out for minced (ground) chillies. After opening, jars should be kept in the refrigerator and the contents consumed by the use-by date.

BELOW: *Crushed chilli flakes*

Crushed chillies

Dried chilli flakes are widely available. Italians call them peperoncini and add them to their famous arrabiata sauce. Sprinkle them on pizzas or add to cooked dishes for a last-minute lift. Crushed dried green jalapeños are a useful pantry item, combining considerable heat with a delicious, melting sweetness.

Chilli paste

It is worth keeping a few jars of ready-made chilli paste, such as harissa or ras-el-hanout, on your shelves. A hot chilli paste is quite easy to make at home. Simply seed fresh chillies, then purée them in a blender or food processor until smooth. Store small amounts in the refrigerator for up to 1 week, or freeze for up to 6 months. Chilli paste can also be made from dried chillies. Having rehydrated them, purée them as you would for fresh chillies. You may have to strain the varieties with tough skins.

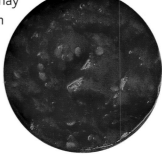
RIGHT: *Hot chilli paste*

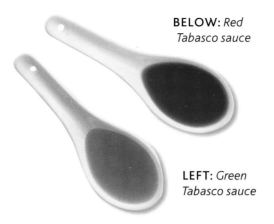

BELOW: *Red Tabasco sauce*

LEFT: *Green Tabasco sauce*

Chilli sauces

There are many varieties of these and the names appear to prove that chillies stimulate the imagination as well as the appetite. Some of the printable ones include Endorphin Rush, Lethal Weapon and Global Warming, and the unforgettable Scorned Woman Hot Sauce.

The most famous chilli sauce, however, is Tabasco, developed in Louisiana by E. McIlhenny in the latter half of the 19th century. Chillies are matured in oak barrels to develop the sauce's unique flavour. Try mixing a

ABOVE:
Sweet chilli sauce (top) and chilli sauce

few drops with fresh lime juice as a baste next time you grill salmon steaks, or add to sauces, soups or casseroles. Also available is Tabasco Jalapeño Sauce – often referred to as green Tabasco sauce. Milder in flavour than the red version, it is good with nachos, hamburgers or on pizza.

Chilli sauces are also widely used in Asia. Chinese chilli sauce is quite hot and spicy, with a hint of fruitiness thanks to the inclusion of apples or plums. For an even milder flavour, look out for sweet chilli sauce, which is a blend of red chillies, sugar and tamarind juice from Sichuan. There is also a thick Chinese sauce made solely from chillies and salt. This is usually sold in jars, and is much hotter than the bottled version. Vietnamese chilli sauce is very hot, while the Thai sauce tends to be thicker and more spicy. Bottled chilli sauces are used both for cooking and as a dip.

Chilli oils

Various types of chilli oil are on sale. Toss them with pasta, add a dash to a stir-fry, or drizzle them over pizzas.

Chilli oils also make a good basis for salad dressings. You can make your own chilli oil by heating chillies in oil, or use a ready-made mixture. Olive oil, flavoured with chipotle and de arbol chillies, with a hint of rosemary, is a particularly good blend. It can also be used for light cooking.

Chilli oil is seldom used for cooking in China and South-east Asia, but is a popular dipping sauce. Two types are widely sold. The first is a simple infusion of dried chillies, onions, garlic

RIGHT:
Chilli oil

and salt in vegetable oil. The second, XO chilli oil, is flavoured with dried scallops and costs considerably more. Chilli oil has a pleasant smell, and a concentrated flavour, much stronger than chilli sauce. It should be used sparingly.

Chilli and Tomato Oil

Heating oil with chillies intensifies the rich flavour. This tastes great sprinkled over fresh pasta.

1 Heat 150ml/^{1}/4 pint/^{2}/3 cup olive oil in a pan. When it is very hot, but not smoking, stir in 10ml/2 tsp tomato purée (paste) and 15ml/ 1 tbsp dried red chilli flakes, then leave to cool in the pan.

2 Pour into an airtight jar and store in the refrigerator for up to 2 months.

Choosing, storing and equipment

Below is some helpful advice on selecting and storing chillies and tips on equipment that will make their preparation simpler.

Choosing and storing

• When buying fresh chillies, apply the same criteria as when buying sweet (bell) peppers. The fruit should look bright and unblemished.

• Avoid any chillies that seem limp or dry, or that have bruising on the skin.

• To store chillies, wrap them in kitchen paper, place in a plastic bag and keep in the salad compartment of the refrigerator for a week or more.

• Chillies can also be frozen. There is no need to blanch them if you plan to use them fairly soon.

• Frozen chillies are a huge boon to the busy cook, as they can be sliced when only partially thawed, and crushed with garlic and ginger to make a fragrant spice paste.

• To dry chillies, thread them on a string, hang them in a warm place until dry, then crush them and store in a sealed jar.

ABOVE: *Chillies dried on string or canes will keep well for many months.*

Equipment

Gloves may not seem an obvious kitchen equipment, but they are invaluable for the dedicated chilli cook. The fine disposable gloves used in hospitals can be used for most chillies, but you need the heavy-duty type for really hot varieties such as habaneros. Of course, you can prepare chillies without wearing gloves, either by using a knife and fork for cutting, or by taking a chance and washing your hands in soapy water afterwards. However, burns from capsaicin, the chemical found in the seeds and fibrous white lining, can be very unpleasant.

A mortar and pestle is ideal for grinding chillies and making chilli pastes, but it does involve a fair amount of hard work. Traditional Indian or Asian granite or stone sets are generally fairly large, with deep, pitted or ridged bowls. The rough surface acts like pumice, increasing the grinding effect. Porous volcanic rock is also used for the Mexican mortar – the molcajete. The Mexican tejolote tends to be shorter than the traditional pestle, and fits neatly into the hand. Molcajetes must be tempered before being used. To do this, a mixture of dry rice and salt is spooned into the bowl, then ground into the surface to remove any loose sand or grit before being discarded.

LEFT: *A smooth mortar and pestle for crushing dry ingredients.*

LEFT: *A rough mortar and pestle for making wet pastes.*

LEFT: *If you like to make your own spice mixtures, then a spice or coffee grinder kept solely for this purpose is very useful.*

A food processor is faster and easier, if less satisfying, than a mortar and pestle, especially for pastes, but must be very carefully cleaned after use. If you intend on preparing chillies and spice pastes frequently, it may be worth investing in a mini food processor, and reserving it for spices.

A spice grinder, or coffee grinder kept specifically for spices, is handy when making dry spice mixtures.

RIGHT: *A food processor or a blender will process chillies very efficiently, and is especially useful for large quantities.*

Preparation and cooking techniques

Every cook handling chillies has experienced the burning, tingling sensation around the sensitive areas of the eyes, nose and mouth. So be warned; be careful. Wear rubber gloves or wash your hands thoroughly in plenty of hot soapy water when handling chillies. Water alone will not remove the chemical capsaicin, and even after using soap, traces may remain. Baby oil or olive oil can be used to remove it from sensitive areas. This advice applies to dried and fresh chillies as the burning properties are equally strong for both.

Preparing fresh chillies

1 If the chilli is to be stuffed, and kept whole, slice the chilli with a sharp knife without separating the two halves. For all other purposes, hold the chilli firmly at the stalk end, and cut it neatly in half lengthways.

2 Cut off the stalk from both halves of the chilli, removing a thin slice containing the stalk from the top of the chilli at the same time. This will help to free the white membrane (placenta) and make it easier to scrape out the seeds to be discarded.

3 Carefully scrape out all the seeds and discard them. Remove the core with a small sharp knife.

4 Cut out any white membrane from the centre of each chilli half. Keep the knife blade close to the flesh so that you can remove all the membrane. This is usually easy to do. Discard the membrane.

5 Slice each piece of chilli into long, thin strips. If diced chilli is needed, line up the strips together in a bunch and cut across the chilli slices to produce tiny pieces.

Soaking dried chillies

Most dried chillies must be rehydrated before being used. This can be done by putting the seeded chillies in a roasting pan in the oven for a few minutes, or by pressing them on to the surface of a hot, dry, heavy frying pan. Do not let them burn, or they could become bitter. Once this is done, continue as below.

1 Wipe the chillies to remove any surface dirt. If you like, you can slit them and shake out the seeds before soaking. Alternatively, just brush away any seeds you can see.

2 Put the chillies in a bowl and pour over hot water to cover. If necessary, fit a saucer in the bowl to keep them submerged. Soak for 20–30 minutes (up to 1 hour if possible), until the colour is restored and the chillies have softened and swelled.

3 Drain the chillies, cut off the stalks if necessary, then slit them and scrape out the seeds. Slice or chop the flesh. If the chillies are to be puréed, process them with a little of the soaking water. Strain the purée if necessary.

Roasting fresh chillies

There are several ways of roasting fresh chillies. You use the grill, roast in the oven, dry-fry as explained below, or hold them over a gas flame.

1 Put the chillies in a dry frying pan and place the pan over the heat until the skins are charred and blistered.

2 For larger chillies that are to be stuffed, use a sharp knife and make a neat slit down the side of each chilli. Then place the chillies in a dry frying pan over a medium heat. Keep turning them frequently until the skins are charred and blistered.

3 Alternatively, roast the chillies in a griddle pan in the oven.

4 To roast chillies on a skewer over a flame, spear them on a long-handled metal skewer and roast them over the flame of a gas burner until the skins blister and darken.

5 Slip the roasted chillies into a strong plastic bag and tie the top to keep the steam in.

6 Set aside for 20 minutes. Take the chillies out of the bag and remove the skins, either by peeling them off, or by rubbing the chillies with a clean dish towel. Cut off the stalks, then slit the chillies and, using a sharp knife, scrape out and discard the seeds.

Making a chilli flower

This makes a very attractive garnish for a special dish.

1 Wearing rubber gloves and using a small pair of scissors or a slim-bladed knife, cut a chilli carefully lengthways from the tip to within 1cm/$\frac{1}{2}$in of the stem end. Repeat this at regular intervals around the chilli.

2 Rinse the chilli in cold water and remove all the seeds. Place in a bowl of iced water and chill for at least 4 hours. For very curly flowers, leave the chilli overnight. When ready to use, lift the chilli out and drain it on kitchen paper.

Grinding chillies

When making chilli powder, this method gives a distinctive and smoky taste.

1 Soak the chillies, if dried, pat dry and then dry-fry in a heavy pan over medium heat until crisp.

2 Transfer to a mortar and grind to a fine powder with a pestle. Store in an airtight container.

Index